SIZE AND DEMOCRACY

THE POLITICS OF THE SMALLER EUROPEAN DEMOCRACIES

Editors

Hans Daalder   *Val R. Lorwin*
Robert A. Dahl   *Stein Rokkan*

SIZE AND DEMOCRACY

Robert A. Dahl and Edward R. Tufte

Stanford University Press, Stanford, California
1973

Stanford University Press
Stanford, California
London: Oxford University Press
© 1973 by the Board of Trustees of the
Leland Stanford Junior University
Printed in the United States of America
ISBN 0-8047-0834-7
LC 72-97200

Acknowledgments

We wish to thank all those, and they were numerous, who read early drafts of our manuscript and provided us with criticism and suggestions. In particular, we are indebted to our colleagues in the study of the smaller European democracies: Hans Daalder, Val Lorwin, and Stein Rokkan. As the reader will discover, the book has been greatly strengthened by data from the Swedish Communal Research Program. For their generosity in providing us with data, and their time, we wish especially to thank Jörgen Westerståhl and his colleagues.

We are grateful to Nancy Hoskins for her care in typing the many revisions of the manuscript and to Joseph Verbalis, Alice-Anne Navin, and Thomas Yunck for research assistance.

A stay at the Center for Advanced Study in the Behavioral Sciences in 1967 enabled us to gather and analyze data and write a first draft. We have received financial support from the Concilium on International Studies of Yale University, the Center of International Studies and the Woodrow Wilson School of Public and International Affairs at Princeton University, the Rockefeller Foundation, the Ford Foundation, and the Christian Michelsen Institute.

Contents

Introduction   1

1. Size and Democracy in Political Thought   4

2. Dimensions of Size and Democracy   17

3. Complexity and Diversity   30

4. Citizen Participation and Sense of Effectiveness   41

5. Citizen Communication and Control   66

6. Competition, Conflict, and Responsiveness   89

7. Size and System Capacity   110

8. Capacity for Independence and Autonomy   118

Epilogue   137

Index   145

Figures

2.1. Two criteria for the ideal democratic polity   21

2.2. Two criteria cut by indifference curves   24

5.1. Population and parliamentary size in 135 countries, 1970   82

5.2. Predicted and actual parliamentary size in 29 democracies, 1970   83

6.1. Hypothetical relation between population size and party competition   101

6.2. Population, population density, percentage of agricultural employment, and political diversity in 25 Swiss cantons, 1959–62   104

6.3. Party competition in 35 states of the United States (the South excluded), 1932–60   107

6.4. Size and the costs of dissent and participation   108

7.1. Foreign trade and population among 124 countries, 1965   114

8.1. Relation between population size and military expenditures for 113 countries   124

8.2. Relation between population size and military expenditures for 32 democracies   125

Tables

3. COMPLEXITY AND DIVERSITY

3.1. Governmental centralization and size in 18 representative democracies   38

4. CITIZEN PARTICIPATION

4.1. Interest in national elections in the United States and the Netherlands   48

4.2. Interest in political parties in the Netherlands and Finland   49

4.3. Organizational membership in five countries   49

4.4. Party membership and electoral activity in Norway and the United States   50

4.5. Political partisanship in Norway, Finland, and the United States   50

4.6. Citizens' expectations of treatment by government officials and the police   52

4.7. Sense of political effectiveness in five countries   53

4.8. Sense of understanding the issues in five countries   54

4.9. Reported impact of governments on daily lives in five countries   56

4.10. Sense of political effectiveness at national and local levels in five countries   58

4.11. Reported attempts to influence the government in five countries   59

4.12. Correlation of political awareness with population size and density in Swedish communes   64

5. CITIZEN COMMUNICATION AND CONTROL

5.1.   Population and parliamentary size, 1970   81
5.2.   Factors influencing parliamentary size in 29 democracies   83
5.3.   Median family income among elected councillors and
       voters, Sweden, 1966   85
5.4.   Positive attitude toward local taxes among Socialist and
       non-Socialist councillors and voters   86

6. COMPETITION, CONFLICT, AND RESPONSIVENESS

6.1.   City size and organizational participation in politics,
       San Francisco Bay Region   98
6.2.   Population size, population density, organizational
       participation in politics, and partisan activity in
       Swedish communes, 1966   99
6.3.   Size, urbanization, and political diversity in the
       Netherlands, municipal elections of 1962   102

7. SIZE AND SYSTEM CAPACITY

7.1.   Population estimates of some large medieval European
       cities   116

8. CAPACITY FOR INDEPENDENCE AND AUTONOMY

8.1.   Simple correlation between population (log) and mili-
       tary expenditures as a per cent of GNP (log) for
       various groups of nations in 1964   123
8.2.   Military expenditures as a per cent of GNP: multiple
       regression analysis   126

SIZE AND DEMOCRACY

Introduction

In 1971 the least populous country with a democratic government was San Marino. Another "small" country, Norway, had 200 times as many people as San Marino; Sweden was more than 400 times larger, the Netherlands 650. Other countries with democratic governments are, of course, much larger than these "small" countries: the United Kingdom has almost 3,000 times as many people as San Marino, the United States about 10,000 times—and India almost 25,000 times! Yet to an Athenian democrat at the time of Pericles, the Netherlands—a "small country"—would seem a gigantic empire, fit only for despotic emperors and slavish citizens. Geneva, during Rousseau's life, had a population of about 22,000.

Are these differences in population or in any other dimension of size—area for example—of any importance? More specifically, is "democracy" related in any way to "size"? How large should a political system be in order to facilitate rational control by its citizens? What are the comparative advantages and disadvantages enjoyed by political systems of different sizes?

Anyone who reflects on these questions will quickly discover that their apparent simplicity conceals a quagmire of complex problems. In searching for answers to the questions as we do in this book, we shall try to confront these problems.

Let us start, then, simply by observing how very relevant these questions are today. Urbanization and the population explosion have raised the specter of uncontrolled growth at all levels of government. In the United States we are particularly concerned with the question of whether it is wise to permit cities—and metropolitan areas and megalopolises—to grow indefinitely. If, as some demographers claim, there now exists one continuous urban area from Virginia to Maine, should we try to turn this into a single vast self-governing megalopolis? Why—or why not? Nation-states are also of varying size. Of many a new state one is tempted to ask whether it is too small to be viable—or too large. There are also concerns about some of the older and better-established democracies. Are the smaller European democracies perhaps too small? Do they need, therefore, to unite in large systems, such as a federal Europe? On the other hand, has the United States with more than 200 million people grown too large? Does it suffer from gigantism and excessive complexity? Is it, in any case, so big that its experience is irrelevant to the rest of the world's countries—where in 1970 about 70 per cent had fewer people than the Netherlands?

As the inexorable thrust of population growth makes a small country large and a large country gigantic, demands are often heard for bringing government closer to the people, for grass-roots democracy. Smaller units are often said to facilitate democracy better than larger units; hence the larger units must be broken up into smaller units, where grass-roots democracy is possible—regions, states, cities, towns, neighborhoods. At the same time, there are complaints that the smaller units are incapable of handling their problems, and demands are heard for larger units such as metropolitan areas, a United States of Europe, a world federation. Concerns are expressed over the size of corporations and the capacities of governments to control them—particularly the international giants.

Thus size enters into the very question of how and indeed whether democratic systems with a high degree of autonomy or sovereignty can survive in a world of great interdependence. Can local governments survive, except as agents of the national government? For that matter, can nations, especially small ones, retain much of their sovereignty? But if every unit surrenders its autonomy to the next larger unit in an ever-ascending series, is there any place left for popular control over government? At the limit, if every smaller unit were simply an agent of a world government and political participation consisted entirely of voting in elections with several billion other citizens, what meaning would be left in the word *democracy*? Conversely, if for at least some kinds of decisions decentralization and autonomy are desirable, the question persists: decentralization to political units of what size?

As we have already suggested, questions about size are made urgent by the rapid growth in population all over the world, for population growth—often accompanied by other social and economic changes—has helped to turn towns into suburbs, suburbs into cities, cities into metropolitan areas, and, in the United States, states into the equivalents of giant countries. The population of California, for example, has come to rival that of Canada, which is larger than that of 80 per cent of the countries of the world. New York City, London, and Tokyo all have more people than about half the countries of the world. The rapid growth of cities has in turn helped to reinforce fears that city life produces larger numbers of relatively isolated, alienated individuals lacking strong ties and a sense of community except when a kind of spurious we-feeling is aroused by highly emotional mass movements. Whether or not these views about mass society are valid, they do call attention to the search for community, and thus to the question of the appropriate political units for expressing one's identity as a member of a community.

ONE

Size and Democracy in Political Thought

Until quite recently—around the end of the eighteenth century —there was little dissent among political philosophers from the view that a democracy or a republic had to be small: a democracy had to be a city-state, by modern standards quite tiny. This view may have been influenced more by accidents of geography than by abstract thought. The Greeks found themselves in a mountainous terrain where the expanding population of a city soon outran the supply of local land for building and cultivation; given the technology of sixth-century Greece, the small, autonomous, distinctly bounded city-state was more necessity than choice. Thus when later philosophers like Plato and Aristotle praised the *polis*, they made a virtue of what once had been necessity. Two thousand years later, Rousseau repeated some of the same themes; and Rousseau, too, had come from a mountainous country where geography pressed inhabitants into isolated peasant villages and towns. Mountainous Italy likewise stimulated the city-state; and though the Romans demonstrated that political and military techniques could prevail over geography, as soon as their stern grip relaxed the terrain of Italy once again encouraged the formation of small states. Geography, then, may have exerted a more profound and arbitrary influence on Western political thought than philosophers like to admit.

However that may be, there is a long and respectable line of thought arguing the virtues of the small polity. Whether they favored or opposed democracy, Greeks of the classical period seem to have agreed that a good polity had to be small in territory and population. Thus Plato, though no democrat, stressed the desirability of a citizen body small enough so that citizens would all know each other and would be as friendly as possible toward one another. He even went so far as to calculate the optimal number of citizens (heads of family) at 5,040.[1]

Aristotle, though not sharing his mentor's passion for numbers, argued that the optimum must lie between a population so small that the polis could not be self-sufficient and so large that the citizens could no longer know one another's characters. He also maintained that all the citizens should be able to assemble at one place and still hear a speaker. Thus the range of the unamplified human voice set a limit.[2]

Whether they favored aristocracy, democracy, or a mixed system, influential Greeks from Pericles to Aristotle seem to have agreed that the polity should be small both in territory and in population. Since this view dominated thinking about democracy for so many centuries, it is worth setting forth in some detail.

A democratic polity must be completely autonomous, because otherwise its citizens could not be fully self-governing: some of their decisions would be limited by the power or authority of individuals or groups outside the citizen body. A democratic polity must have so few citizens that all of them could meet frequently in the popular assembly to listen, to vote, perhaps even to speak. Smallness, it was thought, enhanced the opportunities for participation in and control of the government in many ways. For example, in a small polity every citizen stood a very good chance of being chosen by lot at least once in his lifetime to sit on one of the important administrative bodies. Smallness made it possible for every citizen to know every other, to estimate his qualities, to understand his problems, to develop friendly feelings toward him, to analyze and discuss with comprehension the problems facing the polity. To be sure, if a democratic polity was to be both small and completely autonomous, there was a price to be paid: the citizen body must be self-sufficient and life must be

[1] *Laws*, in *The Dialogues of Plato*, trans. by B. Jowett (New York, 1937), Vol. II: V, 738, 742; VI, 771.
[2] *Politics*, trans. by Ernest Barker (Oxford, 1952), p. 292.

frugal. But frugality was considered a virtue in a democracy, since it helped to reduce inequalities and jealousies among citizens and to toughen them for the rigors of military life, which all must experience from time to time if autonomy was to be maintained.

This view exercised a powerful influence on political theory for two thousand years. In the eighteenth century it still appears in the works of Montesquieu and Rousseau. The preceding paragraph is the very essence of Rousseau. In fact, the small, cohesive, highly consensual city-state peopled by equal and substantially like-minded friends and acquaintances seems so central to Rousseau's vision that applying his views on democracy to the modern nation-state transforms them into a caricature he would probably be the first to reject. To Rousseau, opportunities for citizens to participate effectively in making decisions always vary inversely with size: the larger the number of citizens, the smaller the average citizen's share in the decision. Equality, participation, effective control over government, political rationality, friendliness, and civic consensus all must decline as the population and the territory of the state increase.[3]

Later, the Jacobins found it convenient—necessary, in fact—to divorce Rousseau's general will from its natural setting in the small, consensual city-state and marry it instead to the nation-state. So, too, Americans adopted what they needed from Montesquieu—chiefly his famous principle of dividing the legislative, executive, and judicial powers—and rejected his views on size. Yet Montesquieu's statements about size were highly troubling to his numerous American admirers who wished to construct a new republic of continental proportions.

In *The Spirit of the Laws* Montesquieu argued that it is in the nature of a republic—whether it be a democracy in which the people as a body exercise sovereign power or an aristocracy in which sovereign power resides in the hands of one part of the people—that it have only a small territory and, by implication,

[3] Rousseau's views on size are scattered throughout his works. Like Plato and Aristotle, he often seems to have taken the image of the city-state so much for granted that he did not always make his assumption explicit. However, see *Du Contrat social. Oeuvres choisies de J.-J. Rousseau* (Paris, 1962), I, 5; II, 9–10; III, 1, 3, 4, 13.

a small population. Recapitulating many of the familiar arguments, he held that the requirements of a republican government
—virtue, self-restraint, obedience to law, dedication to the common good, loyalty, equality, frugality—are best met in a republic
of small territory.[4]

> It is in the nature of a republic that it should have a small territory;
> without that, it could scarcely exist. In a large republic, there are large
> fortunes, and consequently little moderation of spirit; there are trusts
> too great to be placed in the hands of any single citizen; interests be-
> come particularized; a man begins to feel that he can be happy, great,
> and glorious without his country; and then, that he can become great
> upon the ruins of his country.
> In a large republic, the common good is sacrificed to a thousand con-
> siderations; it is subordinated to various exceptions; it depends on
> accidents. In a small republic, the public good is more strongly felt,
> better known, and closer to each citizen; abuses are less extensive, and
> consequently less protected.

Montesquieu took the older argument one step further by sug-
gesting that the relation works in both directions. If republics
thrive best in states of very modest dimensions, he maintained,
the converse is also true: in any state as small as a single city, only
a republic can exist. Moreover, the form of government adopted
by any state is closely related to its size.[5]

> If it is the natural property of small states to be governed as republics,
> of middling ones to be governed by monarchs, and of large empires to
> be ruled by despots, it follows that in order to preserve the principles
> of any established government, it is necessary to maintain the existing
> size of the state; and that the nature [*l'esprit*] of the state will change
> to the extent that the state constricts or extends its limits.

By this time in history, however, political philosophers had to
deal with the existence of large nation-states. Montesquieu saw,
as Rousseau did, that the small state could be subjugated by the
large state—which in turn could be destroyed by internal weaknesses. "If a republic is small," wrote Montesquieu, "it is destroyed by an outside force; if it is large, it is destroyed by an

---

4 *De l'Esprit des lois* (Paris, 1961), Vol. I, Book 8, p. 131.
5 *Ibid.*, p. 134.

internal vice."[6] Thus the two-thousand-year-old vision of the democratic city-state contained, for democrats, the elements of a political tragedy: the democratic state, being small, could not preserve the autonomy of its citizens; the large state might preserve autonomy, but only for the rulers, not for the people. One of the central purposes of this book is to explore the nature and reality of this dilemma as it exists today and will probably exist in the foreseeable future.

From Democracy in the City-State to Representative Government in the Nation-State

Less than a century after Rousseau and Montesquieu, the classical city-state view of republican government was, for all practical purposes, dead—the dilemma, so it seemed, solved, the tragedy rewritten with a happy ending. The locus of democracy had shifted from commune, canton, and city-state to nation-state.

Three quite complex series of events in Europe and America helped to bring about this change. First, the rise of nationalism and the nation-state rendered the autonomous commune and the city-state obsolete, or at least virtually impossible either to preserve or to re-create. Henceforth such small units must be subordinated to the nation, and the pride, loyalty, patriotism, and we-feeling that might once have attached primarily or exclusively to them displaced ever more completely to the nation-state. Second, the emergence of elected representative legislatures, particularly in Britain and in the American colonies, furnished an attractive alternative to direct democracy, and thus apparently swept away the constraints of size.

Third, the expanding appeal of popular government encouraged philosophers and ideologues to adapt classical democratic doctrines, implicitly or explicitly, to the grander scale of the nation-state. Montesquieu himself had pointed out that by forming a federation a number of small republics might avoid both the external dangers arising from small size and the internal dangers arising from large size. He cited Holland, Germany, and the Swiss

[6] *Ibid.*, Book 9, p. 137.

League.[7] But representative government in the nation-state led to an even sharper break with classical tradition than Montesquieu envisaged. Destutt de Tracy, a French thinker whose criticism of Montesquieu profoundly influenced Thomas Jefferson, argued that direct democracy was feasible only in primitive societies; elsewhere, as in Greece, it was short-lived and not really democratic. According to Destutt, representative government made Montesquieu and the whole classical tradition obsolete: "Representation, or representative government, may be considered as a new invention, unknown in Montesquieu's time. . . . Representative democracy . . . is democracy rendered practicable for a long time and over a great extent of territory."[8]

At the American Constitutional Convention in 1787, however, the issue of size was still alive. Montesquieu's federation of republics had been tried out under the Articles of Confederation and, in the view of most of the Convention delegates, found wanting. A *national* republic was now needed in order to govern what many delegates rightly predicted would one day be an immense territory with perhaps a hundred million citizens. Yet so authoritative was the classical insistence on small polities that on no question they confronted were the delegates more pessimistic than on the long-run prospects for republican government on such a scale.[9] Predictably, their opponents contended that a republic with such a large territory inhabited by such a heterogeneous

---

[7] *Ibid.*, p. 138.

[8] *A Commentary and Review of Montesquieu's Spirit of Laws* (Philadelphia, 1811), p. 19, cited in Adrienne Koch, *The Philosophy of Thomas Jefferson* (Chicago, 1964), pp. 152, 157. Destutt was not alone in thinking that the representative system could transform popular government. James Mill wrote in 1820, "In the grand discovery of modern times, the system of representation, the solution of all difficulties, both speculative and practical, will perhaps be found." Cited in George H. Sabine, *History of Political Theory*, 3d ed. (New York, 1961), p. 695. And Madison wrote in a letter of 1833, "The introduction of the representative principle into modern Governments . . . has shown the practicability of popular governments in a larger sphere, and that the enlargement of the sphere was a cure for many of the evils inseparable from the popular forms in small communities." Saul K. Padover, ed., *The Forging of American Federalism, Selected Writings of James Madison* (New York, 1965), p. 63.

[9] See, for example, the views of Ellsworth, Hamilton, Wilson, and Gouverneur Morris, as reported by Madison in *Documents Illustrative of the Formation of the Union of the American States* (Washington, D.C., 1927), pp. 219–20, 274, 276, 408.

population was "an absurdity, and contrary to the whole experience of mankind."[10]

Several numbers of *The Federalist* were devoted to the problems of size.[11] In Federalist No. 9, Hamilton remarked that "the opponents of the plan proposed have, with great assiduity, cited and circulated the observations of Montesquieu on the necessity of a contracted territory for republican government." By way of rebuttal Hamilton quoted Montesquieu at some length on the advantages of a confederated republic, somewhat disingenuously describing Montesquieu's statement as "a luminous abridgment of the principal arguments in favor of the Union."[12]

But it was Madison who provided the most sophisticated rebuttal of the classical view. In a famous argument set forth during the Constitutional Convention and used again in Federalist No. 10, Madison met the classical position head on and triumphantly turned it around. Far from being a disadvantage to a republic, Madison contended, size was actually an advantage—indeed a necessity. His argument is worth setting forth at some length.

A supreme danger in any democracy, Madison insisted, is the possibility that a passionate majority might "sacrifice to its ruling passion or interest both the public good and the rights of other citizens. To secure the public good and private rights against the danger of such a faction, and at the same time to preserve the spirit and the form of popular government, is then the great object to which our inquiries are directed. Let me add that it is the great desideratum by which this form of government can be rescued from the opprobrium under which it has so long labored, and be recommended to the esteem and adoption of mankind. . . ." Yet where a small, direct democracy along classical lines "can admit of no cure for the mischiefs of faction," a representative republic "opens a different prospect, and promises the cure for which we are seeking." The greater the size, the greater the "variety of parties and interests," and hence the less the probabil-

---

[10] Cf. Cecelia M. Kenyon, ed., *The Antifederalists* (New York, 1966), pp. xxxix–xlviii; also Jackson Turner Main, *The Antifederalists, Critics of the Constitution* (Chapel Hill, N.C., 1961), p. 129.

[11] Nos. 10, 14, 55, 56, and 58, among others.

[12] B. F. Wright, ed., *The Federalist* (Cambridge, Mass., 1961), pp. 126, 127.

ity "that a majority of the whole will have a common motive to invade the rights of other citizens; or if such a common motive exists, it will be more difficult for all who feel it to discover their own strength, and to act in unison with each other. . . . Hence, it clearly appears, that the same advantages which a [representative] republic has over a [direct] democracy, in controlling the effects of faction, is enjoyed by a large over a small [representative] republic,—is enjoyed by the Union over the states composing it. . . .

"The influence of factious leaders may kindle a flame within their particular States, but will be unable to spread a general conflagration through the other States. . . .

"In the extent and proper structure of the Union, therefore, we behold a republican remedy for the diseases most incident to a republican government."[13]

We have dwelt at length on the controversy over size in the early history of the United States precisely because it is the first major confrontation of the classical view with the emerging doctrines and practices of representative government on a national scale. If there are historical watersheds, surely here was one. Thenceforth, the United States seemed a standing refutation of the classical position on popular government. Whether the classical arguments were actually refuted by American experience is, as we shall see in a moment, doubtful. But the longer the United States persisted, the more foolish it seemed to argue that a representative republic—and thus a kind of democracy—could not exist in a large country.

The subsequent history of the controversy is worthy of a monograph (surprisingly, none exists), but since our primary aim here is to present theory and findings rather than intellectual history, the briefest summary will have to serve. The French Revolution was the first European attempt to create a democratic republic on a national scale. The Jacobins preached and practiced centralization; swept away the old intervening, decentralizing institutions; interpreted the general will as the nation's will, not the rich multiplicity of local wills; and during the height of their rule

13 *Ibid.*, pp. 133–36.

claimed (in a fashion more familiar in the twentieth century) exclusive knowledge of what that will demanded.

The failure of the French Revolution to produce a durable democratic republic did not halt the three historical changes mentioned earlier. If the classical arguments were not refuted, more and more they were ignored. Nationalism and the nation-state, representative institutions, and growing support for popular government simply pushed them aside. John Stuart Mill is a perfect symbol of this change. In a chapter in his *Representative Government* entitled "The Ideally Best Form of Government," Mill seeks to show that "the only government which can fully satisfy all the exigencies of the social state is one *in which the whole people participate*" (emphasis added). Then, almost as an afterthought, he concludes his chapter with this pregnant sentence: "But since all cannot, in a community exceeding a single small town, participate personally in any but very minor portions of the public business, it follows that the ideal type of a perfect government must be representative." In this one sentence, Mill casually dismisses the classical view as irrelevant to the modern world.

By the middle of the nineteenth century, then, the older conception of democracy as suited only to the city-state had almost wholly lost its force. Democratic doctrines were now thoroughly adapted to nationalism, the nation-state, and representative government. The Philosophical Radicals and later the liberals in England, Andrew Jackson and Abraham Lincoln in the United States, Mazzini and Garibaldi in Italy, Michelet in France—all expounded the newer view.

Main Claims and Counterclaims

Nonetheless, the classical conception of the relationship between size and popular government has not completely vanished from Western thought. It has survived as a model, familiar at least to some scholars. And the idea that democracy is somehow linked with smallness has retained considerable appeal. Opponents of centralization, supporters of local government, advocates of grass-roots or participatory democracy, spokesmen for decentralization in various forms, all have continued to defend the special virtues of democracy in the smaller territorial units as well as in cooperatives, firms, industries, educational institutions, and the like.

To provide a comprehensive overview of this continuing controversy, we shall set forth the main claims and counterclaims that have explicitly or implicitly characterized it, from classical political theory to recent theories about social conflict and small-group theory. It is convenient at this point to ignore definitional problems. In particular, we leave "smaller," "larger," and "democracy" undefined for the moment.

*

ON CITIZEN PARTICIPATION

1. Smaller democracies provide more opportunity for citizens to participate effectively in decisions.

2. *But*: Larger democracies provide opportunities for citizens to participate, at least by voting in elections, in the decisions of a political system large enough to control all or most of the major aspects of their situation that can be controlled.

ON SECURITY AND ORDER

3. Smaller democracies make it easier for citizens to internalize norms and values, hence to increase voluntary compliance and reduce coercion.

4. *But*: Larger democracies provide an opportunity to extend the rule of law (as opposed to violence among states) over a larger area.

5. *And*: Larger democracies are better equipped to prevent damage to the internal life of the society from outside forces—such as invasion and economic threats.

ON UNITY AND DIVERSITY

6. Smaller democracies are likely to be more nearly homogeneous with respect to beliefs, values, and goals.

7. *Conversely*: Larger democracies are likely to exhibit more

diversity in beliefs, values, goals, social and economic characteristics, occupations, etc.

ON THE COMMON INTEREST

8. Smaller democracies make it easier for a citizen to perceive
a relation between his own self-interest or understanding of the
good and a public or general interest, the interests of others, or
general conceptions of the good.

9. *Conversely*: Larger democracies provide more opportunity
for divergence of views on individual, group, and general interests and goals.

10. *And*: Larger democracies reduce the likelihood that a
single interest of one segment of the members will dominate the
whole system (as happens, for example, in company towns).

ON LOYALTIES

11. Smaller democracies are more likely to generate loyalty to
a single integrated community.

12. *Conversely*: Larger democracies are more likely to generate
multiple loyalties to various "communities."

ON EMOTIONAL LIFE

13. Citizens of smaller democracies are more likely to invest
civic relationships with high levels of affect.

14. *Conversely*: Citizens of larger democracies are more likely
to divest civic relations of affect, to make civic relations more impersonal and emotionally neutral.

15. The citizens of smaller democracies are likely to consider
each other friends or enemies, according to whether they agree
or disagree on politics.

16. *Conversely*: The citizens of larger democracies are less
likely to consider their fellow citizens either friends or enemies
for political reasons.

17. Smaller democracies produce stronger pressures for conformity to collective norms.

18. *Conversely*: Larger democracies weaken pressures for conformity to collective norms.

19. *But*: Alienation and anomie—loss of community—are much more likely in larger democracies.

ON RATIONALITY

20. Smaller democracies make possible greater speed and accuracy of communication among all members of the system.

21. *And*: Smaller democracies provide more opportunities for all citizens to gain knowledge needed for decisions by direct observation and experience.

22. *But*: Larger democracies provide more opportunities for all citizens, acting collectively, to exercise control over a broader range of important matters—and hence over their situation.

23. *And*: Larger democracies provide greater opportunities for individuals to develop specialized skills, hence to develop skills needed for rational solutions to problems.

24. In general, then, citizens in a smaller democracy are likely to understand their political problems better than citizens in a larger democracy (consider propositions 1, 6, 8, 20, and 21).

25. *On the contrary*, citizens in a larger democracy have greater opportunities for exploring a bigger set of alternatives than citizens in a smaller democracy; hence *they* are the more likely to understand their political problems better and to control their situations more completely (consider propositions 2, 4, 5, 9, 10, 12, 16, 17, 22, and 23).

ON CONTROL OF LEADERS

26. Leaders are likely to be more responsive to citizen views in smaller democracies (consider propositions 1, 3, 6, 8, 11).

27. *On the contrary*, leaders are likely to be more responsive to citizen views in *larger* democracies (consider propositions 10, 16, 18).

*

Two aspects of this presentation of claims and counterclaims are worth noting. First, most of the claims and counterclaims are perfectly consistent with one another. Indeed, it is not until we get down to the last four summary propositions (24–27) that the statements are actually contradictory.

Second, most of the statements can be interpreted at the explicit level as factual assertions or hypotheses, e.g. "Citizens of smaller democracies are more likely to invest civic relationships with high levels of affect." This is not, on its face, an evaluation. If it were assumed to be factually correct, its evaluation would depend upon the value criteria used. In some cases, the relevant criteria of value are obvious and not likely to be controversial. Thus, if proposition 3 is factually correct, most people would doubtless be prepared to mark up a point for the smaller democracies. In practice, however, the value criteria are often obscure or controversial; what is more, the facts themselves are frequently in doubt.

In the chapters that follow, we hope to establish on firmer ground both the factual and the valuational foundations of the propositions involved in the ancient and continuing controversy over size and democracy.

TWO

Dimensions of Size and Democracy

A territorial entity has several dimensions of size: population, area, density, and others. Most discussions of the relation between size and popular government use population as their criterion of size, but even this may be ambiguous, for a writer may have in mind all inhabitants, all citizens, all adults, eligible voters, or only actual voters. Plato's optimal population, for example, referred to citizens in the Greek sense of free adult males; hence it excluded women, minors, foreigners, and slaves. In a direct democracy, the most relevant aspect of population size is generally the number of citizens eligible to attend meetings of the assembly —a small part of the total population. In a representative system each of the other aspects may be relevant for some purposes.

Some propositions about size and popular government use area as their criterion of size. The classical view of the polis, whether democratic or aristocratic, required a small population within a small area: "What was said above of the population—that it should be such as to be surveyable—is equally true of the territory."[1] To be sure, population and territory tend to be related. In 1965, among 136 countries, the correlation between total population and total area was 0.69. Yet this correlation conceals extreme variations. The world's seven largest countries, listed in order of decreasing area, are the USSR, Canada, China, the United States, Brazil, Australia, and India. Of the four representative democracies in this group of giant countries, two—Canada and Australia—are relatively small in population, and two—In-

[1] Aristotle, *Politics*, trans. by Ernest Barker (Oxford, 1952), p. 293.

dia and the United States—are respectively the second and fourth most populous countries in the world.

Occasionally, size refers to population density, that is, the number of people per square kilometer of territory (or perhaps of arable land). In discussions using this dimension of size, for instance, the Netherlands might be considered less likely than Norway to grant extensive local autonomy, because the spillover effects of local actions on roads, highways, public health, and the like would be much more pronounced in a densely populated country than in a country of widely separated villages.

This comparison suggests still another relevant dimension of size: the distribution of the population. We have already noted that the classical preference for the autonomous city-state may have been shaped by the geography of Greece, which tended to force the population into villages and cities more or less sharply delimited by sea, mountains, or other natural features. In some countries, the population is distributed among a large number of relatively small cities and towns. Thus 70 per cent of the Swiss people live in towns and villages with fewer than 20,000 inhabitants. In the United Kingdom, the distribution is almost the reverse: two-thirds live in cities with more than 20,000 inhabitants. Yet—to make a different comparison—only 7 per cent of all Britons live in London, whereas one-fourth of all Austrians live in Vienna.[2]

Most discussions of the relation between size and democracy refer explicitly or implicitly to *absolute size*: the number of people, the number of square miles, the percentage of the population in cities of more than 20,000 people, and the like. But absolute size is sometimes less significant than relative size, particularly in international relations. If all of Europe except Belgium consisted of city-states, Belgium would be a great power and would probably never be invaded. But alongside Germany and France it is a small power, twice overrun in this century. Obviously, too, Finland's international position would be different if it did not have a giant country like the USSR as a neighbor. When we come to

2 Data from E. A. G. Robinson, *Economic Consequences of the Size of Nations* (London, 1960), p. 178.

discuss the viability of small democracies, we shall have to consider not only absolute but also relative size.

Finally, change in size is sometimes important. At the end of the First World War, Austria, "the former central province of an empire of 50 million suddenly shrank to an independent country of some 6 1/2 million inhabitants faced by quickly growing tariff walls around its former markets. . . . The question of size overshadowed all other problems. The shock of being reduced from a big to a small country resulted in a very acute size pessimism, particularly among the articulate middle classes who, after having lost some of their well-protected job opportunities, tended to take an equally poor view of the nation's chances as they took of their own."[3]

Socioeconomic Characteristics as Dimensions of Size

Size can also be looked at from a socioeconomic point of view. We might, for example, choose to measure the size of a country by its gross national product (GNP) per capita. Such a choice seems attractive because previous studies have demonstrated a clear correlation between the frequency of representative democracy and such highly intercorrelated socioeconomic variables as urbanization, industrialization, and per capita GNP.[4] In our own analysis we also find that levels of socioeconomic development are independent of total population and only weakly related to total area and average density. Why not abandon these more conventional measures of size, therefore, and use socioeconomic variables instead?

Although looking at size in this way would have advantages, to substitute socioeconomic indicators for conventional measures would not clarify the issues involved in the historic controversy over size and democracy. It would only transform the problem into a different one. The relationship between representative democracy and various socioeconomic variables is important in its

[3] K. W. Rothschild, "Size and Viability: The Lesson of Austria," in Robinson, pp. 168–69.

[4] Robert A. Dahl, *Polyarchy: Participation and Opposition* (New Haven, 1971), p. 63. See also the studies cited in footnotes 1–3 of the same book, pp. 62–63.

own right, and has received a good deal of attention. But that relationship is not the one primarily at issue here.

However, when we deal with the capabilities of a political system, as we shall do in the last chapter, we shall have to concern ourselves with socioeconomic variables, for a nation's capacity for survival, effectiveness, and autonomy appears to be more dependent on the size of some of its key resources (wealth, trade, skilled workers, college graduates, etc.) than on the size of its population or territory. Elsewhere for the most part we will use population or population-related indicators.[5] To avoid confusion, however, we shall always specify the particular indicator we are using.

Some Dimensions of Democracy

Having defined size by several of the most relevant dimensions, we must now do the same for democracy. The two traditions, one locating democracy in the city-state, the other in the nation-state, appear to share some common elements. In both traditions, the ideal polity could be described as one that satisfies at least two criteria:

> the criterion of *citizen effectiveness* (citizens acting responsibly and competently fully control the decisions of the polity); and
>
> the criterion of *system capacity* (the polity has the capacity to respond fully to the collective preferences of its citizens).

To clarify the relation between these criteria and the two traditions of democracy, we illustrate them in Figure 2.1. Since any system is better than another if it is better by one criterion and not worse by the other, clearly a system at point *a* would be better than systems at *b, c,* or *d.* As we shall see in the last chapter, some of the most critical problems of evaluating the impacts of size on democracy today arise because of conflicts between the two criteria. For example, how would we choose among systems at *b, c,* and *d?*

---

[5] Because distribution of units by population are usually highly skewed, we shall ordinarily use the logarithm to the base ten of the population.

Now the *classical* tradition of democratic thought held, in effect, that the small, autonomous, democratic city-state was at *a*; that is, it was better, according to these two criteria, than any alternative polity. Any other system would necessarily be lower on the scale of citizen effectiveness and could not, in the best of circumstances, have any greater capacity than the city-state for providing all the requirements of a good life. In this view, the democratic city-state was better because, and to the extent that, it more fully satisfied the criteria of citizen effectiveness and system capacity. The requirements for meeting the two criteria were interpreted in the following way:

Citizen effectiveness. (1) In order for citizens fully to control the decisions of the polity, they must participate directly in making those decisions. (2) In order to participate directly in making decisions, the number of citizens must be very small.

System capacity. If the polity is to have the capacity to respond fully to its citizens, it must be completely autonomous or sovereign.

Thus the requirements for meeting the two criteria emphasized by the classical tradition were direct participation by the citizens (participatory democracy) and complete autonomy for the polity (i.e., for the whole body of citizens). Obviously even this tradition does not envision a polity exempt from the laws of nature, from moral law, or from the intervention of the gods. Nor does it envision a polity utterly unaffected by the actions of other autonomous polities. But in the classical perspective no person outside the small citizen body had any legitimate claim to intervene in the governing of the city-state.

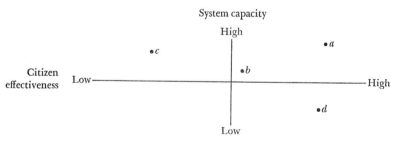

Fig. 2.1. Two criteria for the ideal democratic polity.

When the idea of democracy was displaced to the nation-state, the requirements for satisfying the criteria were radically altered:

System capacity. (1) Only the nation-state has the capacity to respond fully to collective preferences. (2) Therefore the nation-state (but no smaller units) should be completely autonomous.

Citizen effectiveness. (1) Nation-states are too large for citizens to participate directly in all or even most decisions. (2) Therefore, citizens must be able to participate in decisions at least indirectly, typically by electing representatives or delegates to decision-making offices.

Note that the restraints on size that were central to the classical tradition and the requirement of direct participation were both eliminated. And, foreshadowing a further change that we shall discuss in a moment, even the requirement of autonomy was weakened. Smaller units might, and undoubtedly would, exist within an independent nation-state that had a representative government at the national level. Citizens might, and probably would, expect these smaller units also to be, in some sense, democratic. Yet unless the nation-state were dismantled, the smaller units could not be fully autonomous.

Thus, as the criteria for democracy were expanded—or weakened, depending on one's point of view—the universe of systems called democratic became larger and more heterogeneous. This universe contained four significantly different types of systems: (1) those, like Athens in the fifth century B.C., in which participation is direct and autonomy is complete, (2) those, like the New England town and the small Swiss canton, in which participation is direct but autonomy is partial, (3) those, like the nineteenth-century nation-states with representative governments, in which autonomy is complete but participation is indirect, and (4) those, like subnational units with representative governments, in which autonomy is partial and participation is indirect.

With the possible exception of a few surviving preliterate societies, category 1 seems to have no contemporary members. When we search for relevant examples of direct democracy today, we must turn to subordinate units of government—a New England town with its town meeting, a small Swiss canton with its *Lands-*

gemeinde; that is, to systems in category 2—or to devices for direct participation within a representative system, such as initiative, referendum, and recall. And it is obvious that at the national level even Switzerland, which uses the initiative and the referendum, falls into category 3; whereas representative systems at local, state, cantonal, and provincial levels fall into category 4. Throughout the civilized world, then, we can find no political system that combines sovereignty with full-scale direct participation; the two characteristics that together define category 1 have become separated. Independent nation-states may be more or less sovereign, but they do not operate wholly, or even mostly, by direct participation. A few units of government like the New England town or the smaller Swiss cantons may be governed more or less by direct participation, but they are subordinate units of government, not sovereign.

The depletion of category 1 has taken place in two stages, one completed, the other well under way. In the first stage, as we have seen, the effort to adapt democratic ideas to the nation-state brings about a shift in both theory and practice from direct to indirect systems of participation—from category 1 to category 3.

This shift in perspective has come about, at least in part, because the two basic criteria come into conflict with one another. In these circumstances, a reasonable person who wishes his polity to measure up to both criteria might, and indeed surely would, have to consider the trade-offs. A rational or reasonable democrat who wished to maximize the chances of attaining certain of his goals might well trade some loss of personal effectiveness for some gain in the capacity of the system to attain them. To offer a hypothetical case, let us assume, without arguing the matter, that the capacity to reduce pollution in Lake Michigan is, up to some threshold, a function of size. A citizen who wants the lake cleaned up might well reason as follows: If the authority to deal with pollution is left to local governments, the job is unlikely to be accomplished even if a majority of people around the lake—not to say in the whole country—would like it cleaned up. For those favoring vigorous pollution control may be in a minority in some towns. Consequently that town will probably continue to pollute the lake. Thus only a regional or perhaps even a federal agency, responsible to regional or national opinion, can be effective. Of course I am bound to have only negligible influence on the decisions of such an agency, whereas I might be highly influential in my own town. Nonetheless, on balance I prefer the agency to the present system of decentralized and uncoordinated units.

To represent the matter more abstractly, we might imagine that our earlier graph is now cut by indifference curves, *A, B, C,* etc., as in Figure 2.2. Our citizen reasoning about pollution would regard any polity along line *A*, for example, as equally satisfactory. In the southeast direction along line *A*, what he gains in personal effectiveness he loses in the capacity of the system to solve the problem at hand. However, any system on line *A* would be preferable to any system on line *B*, any system on *B* would be preferable to any on *C*, etc.

In the second stage, which is now taking place, the nation-state itself becomes inadequate and is gradually transformed into a kind of local government within a larger international system. Thus, just as category 1 was emptied as the autonomous city-state disappeared, so category 3 will be emptied as the autonomous nation-state disappears. Even the nation-state, then, will move from category 3 to category 4.

The tendency for members of categories 1 and 3 to vanish is associated with a shift in the interpretation of the second basic criterion of democracy. The concept of a polity or political system no longer refers to a single integral unit but to a complex entity consisting of a number of interrelated units, some subordinate or partly subordinate to others. The unitary polity has be-

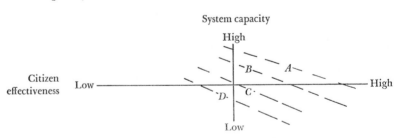

Fig. 2.2. Two criteria cut by indifference curves.

come the complex polity. In order to satisfy the two democratic criteria, and particularly the criterion of system capacity, the requirements evidently have to be reformulated yet another time.

System capacity: (1) Only a complex polity consisting of a number of interrelated political units above and below the level of the nation-state has the capacity to respond adequately to the collective preferences of citizens of nation-states. (2) Therefore units at and below the level of the nation-state should not be wholly autonomous.

Citizen effectiveness: No single method for maximizing citizen effectiveness within each of these units is best. In some, direct participation is best; in some the election of representatives; in others, more indirect methods, including delegation of authority to officials appointed by national governments.

Problems of Terminology

Should the same word, democracy, be applied to systems as radically different as the city-state and the nation-state? The multi-unit polity, particularly one in which the nation-state itself loses its autonomy, stretches the term even more.

Clarity would have been better served if the term "democracy" had never been transferred from ideals and institutions associated with direct popular rule in the city-state to the ideals and institutions associated with representative government in the nation-state. The two types of political system are far too different to lie easily together in one category. It is almost as if the poverty of our nomenclature had compelled us to put modern representative government in the same category as the mixed parliamentary monarchy of eighteenth-century England; for although the two kinds of system do have a great deal in common, their differences are as interesting and significant as their similarities. Stretching the term has not only hampered the creation of more fruitful ways of classifying political systems; joining the older notions of democracy to the theory and practice of modern representative government has also introduced so wide a disparity, not simply between ideal and reality but between ideal and potential, as to generate false hopes, despair, and cynicism. For of course in a large nation-state the people cannot even rule in quite the same way or to the same extent that they might under optimal conditions in a small city.

However, attempts to maintain terminological distinctions among drastically different variants of "democracy" have largely failed. In Federalist No. 10 Madison tried to restrict the term "democracy" to a "pure democracy, by which I mean a society consisting of a small number of citizens, who assemble and administer the government in person," and to reserve the term "republic" for "a government in which the scheme of representation takes place." Unfortunately for Madison, as he surely knew, his proposal had no historical justification. The Roman Republic, after all, had failed to develop representative institutions. The 800-year-old Republic of Venice, then in its last decade of existence, was an aristocratic government in which all male members of the aristocracy participated directly through the Grand Council. Curiously, Madison's definitions even ran directly counter to the authority of Montesquieu; we must assume that Madison was acquainted with Montesquieu's description of a republic and his distinction between the two kinds of republic—a democracy, in which the "body of the people is possessed of the supreme power," and an aristocracy, in which "the supreme power is lodged in the hands of a part of the people."[6] His friend and political ally Jefferson, on the other hand, defined the term "republic" exactly as Madison had defined "pure democracy." Governments could be thought of as having a greater or lesser degree of republicanism, or as we might say, democracy. A representative government, then, could be "more or less republican, in proportion as it has in its composition more or less of this ingredient of the direct action of the citizens."[7] This was a useful conception; but the up-

[6] *De l'Esprit des lois* (Paris, 1961), Vol. I, Book II, p. 12. Although Madison's proposed usage of "democracy" corresponds exactly with Rousseau's in *The Social Contract*, his definition of "republic" diverges from both Rousseau and Montesquieu.

[7] In a letter to John Tyler in 1810, Jefferson wrote, "Were I to assign to this term [republic] a precise and definite idea, I would say, purely and simply, it means a government by its citizens in mass, acting directly and personally, according to rules established by the majority; and that every other government is more or less republican, in proportion as it has in its composition more or less of this ingredient

shot was that Madison's attempt to distinguish terminologically between a simple or direct "democracy" and an indirect or representative "republic" did not prevail.

Jefferson's mentor, Destutt de Tracy, had used the term "representative democracy."[8] Madison and Jefferson may have preferred the term "republic" partly for political reasons: they may have wished to blunt the opposition of some critics of the new system to whom the word democracy was less respectable than the word republic. Nonetheless, the terminological distinction between direct democracy and representative democracy later became fairly widely accepted, at least among those who thought about the matter at all. Yet with the further passage of time representative democracy became simply democracy, and the radical differences between the two were often obscured, even in scholarly writings, by the implication of the single label that they were both fundamentally the same. Different labels would have called attention to the alternative possibility that they might be fundamentally different.[9]

Beyond Terminology

The argument over size and democracy is, of course, more than a matter of terminology or classification. As we have seen in these first two chapters, the argument persists because of disagreements over the extent to which the benefits of "large" units outweigh the costs; or, to state the same criterion from the opposite perspective, the extent to which the benefits of "small" units out-

---

of the direct action of the citizens. *Such a government is evidently restrained to very narrow limits of space and population. I doubt if it would be practicable beyond the extent of a New England township.*" Quoted in Adrienne Koch, *The Philosophy of Thomas Jefferson* (New York, 1950), p. 165. Emphasis added by the present authors.

[8] *Ibid.*, p. 157.

[9] In an attempt to reduce this confusion, one of the authors has in several books reintroduced the old term *polyarchy* as a substitute for representative democracy. The *Oxford English Dictionary* gives its meaning as "the government of a state or city by many; contrasted with monarchy." The earliest cited usage in English is 1609. However, because its usage here would require a more extended definition than is strictly necessary to the argument later on, and out of deference to readers who resist what appears, wrongly, to be a neologism, we have not used the word in this book.

weigh the costs. Not many people doubt that there are *some* advantages to smallness and *some* disadvantages; nor do many contest the fact that great size has both costs and benefits. The controversy is over the relative magnitudes. Advocates of the classical view contend that the small, autonomous unit is truly optimal for the good life; whatever gains might accrue to larger units are bound to be offset by disadvantages. Advocates of representative government in the nation-state make precisely the opposite assessment of the relative costs and gains.

Those who advocate a complex polity of interrelated units oppose both views and contend that the either/or debate is fundamentally misleading. The balance of advantage will favor a unit of one size for some purposes and a unit of a different size for other purposes. No single unit size will be optimal for every purpose. An emergent complex polity of interrelated units will need units that change in size and scope as technology, communications, values, identifications, and other factors alter the balance of gains and costs.

Because of its origins, democratic theory has not yet adjusted to the complex polity. We are a long way indeed from knowing how to create a fluid, adaptive, complex polity. Among other things we are handicapped because we do not have much reliable information on the costs and gains associated with popular governments of different size and scope.

In what follows we make a beginning. We consider questions of size and democracy at both national and subnational levels. We therefore make comparisons within and among countries. Since an assessment of size and democracy has not been attempted before in any systematic way, our results are pretty limited. We specify some of the questions that ought to be asked, at least by anyone operating from a democratic perspective. There are, we realize, other relevant perspectives and other relevant questions. Though we try to provide answers to the questions we pose, limitations of data are often overwhelming. When we cannot go much beyond theory because we lack good data, we nonetheless make an effort to formulate theory in such a way as to help future investigators.

In the following chapters, then, our inquiry is guided by the two criteria of democracy elaborated and qualified in this chapter. With respect to the first criterion, *citizen effectiveness,* we ask whether the size of the polity has significant consequences for the following areas:

> The complexity of political life, and hence the capacity of citizens to act responsibly and competently in achieving their goals (Chapter 4).
>
> The opportunities available to citizens to participate in political life and their incentives to do so (Chapter 5).
>
> Their capacities for accurately communicating their goals and preferences to decision makers (Chapter 6).
>
> The incentives of decision makers to respond to the preferences of citizens (Chapter 7).

Although the second basic criterion is a minor theme in all the chapters, it is not directly discussed until Chapter 8. In that chapter we examine the consequences of size for the *capacity of the system* to respond fully to the collective preferences of its citizens. We also consider further in Chapter 8 the problem of conflict between the two basic criteria and the existence of trade-offs between system capacity and citizen effectiveness.

THREE

Complexity and Diversity

When the domestic achievements of some of the smaller democracies are offered as a model for the United States, a frequent response is: "Ah, but those countries are smaller and less complex; consequently their problems are simpler." Is it true that smaller countries are in some sense simpler, less complex than larger countries? Are larger units within a country also more complex than smaller ones? If so, what difference does this make in the political life of the countries or units in question?

The concept of complexity is itself complex and elusive. Generally speaking, a system might be said to be more complex (1) the greater the number of variables that have to be taken into account in order to understand, explain, or predict the behavior of the system, or (2) the greater the variation in the relationships among these variables, or both. If system A contains not only more variables than system B but also more variation in the relationships among them, most people would probably agree that A is more complex than B. Problems arise, however, if A is more complex than B by the first criterion, but less complex than B by the second.

A political system might be said to be more complex (1) the greater the number of categories of actors whose attitudes, interests, wants, preferences, demands, and goals have to be taken into account, and (2) the greater the variation in their attitudes.

At present it appears impossible to compare many nations on the basis of the second criterion, and data for making comparisons within nations are poor. Even the first criterion is hard to apply, for it is difficult to say which actors are politically relevant and have to be taken into account, and what their attitudes, interests, and the like may be.

Categoric Diversity

There are a number of categories, however, that social scientists typically try to take into account in analyzing a political system: occupation, income, social status, religion, language, region, and the like. With respect to any one of these categories, a political system might be considered more diverse or heterogeneous (1) the greater the number of subsets into which the population is divided, or (2) the more nearly the subsets approach each other in size, or both. Again, there is the potential problem of a system that is more complex by one criterion and less complex by the other. Here, we propose to call a difference on either dimension a difference in *categoric diversity*.[1]

Although categoric diversity is obviously only one element in complexity, it has the advantage of being accessible to study. Categoric diversity can be measured in several ways. One way that is simple, intuitively appealing, and sometimes more valid than complex measures is to calculate the proportion of the population falling into the largest subgroup of a particular category. For example, a country in which 90 per cent of the population speak the same language would be considered less diverse with respect to language than a country in which the largest language group consists of only 30 per cent of the population.

As we shall see, it is useful to distinguish two kinds of categoric diversity: *cultural diversity* (variation in language, religion, race, or region) and *socioeconomic diversity* (variation in occupation, education, income, wealth, and the like). These two kinds of categoric diversity are related in somewhat different ways to three sets of determining conditions: unique historical factors, socioeconomic level, and size.

To explain why some countries contain more sharply differen-

---

[1] In *The Analysis of Political Cleavages* (New Haven, 1970), chap. 3, Douglas W. Rae and Michael Taylor develop measures for this concept, which they call fragmentation.

tiated subcultures than others, we usually need to turn to historical factors. Take language, for example. While some countries
are linguistically divided, others are linguistically homogeneous.
The entire explanation seems to lie with their historical legacies.
Thus Switzerland has four significant languages, Belgium and
Finland each have two, and for all practical purposes the Netherlands and Sweden each have only one. These differences in linguistic diversity have virtually nothing to do with size or economic development. France with five times the population of
Belgium, West Germany with six times, or the United States with
more than twenty times, are all much more homogeneous linguistically. The explanation is not to be found in either the size
of a country or the level of economic development but in the fact
that several peoples already divided by ancient and extraordinarily durable differences in language were in the course of history united within the boundaries of one country. Writing of
Belgium, Lorwin has remarked that "the nation born in 1830
was bisected by an internal linguistic frontier which had hardly
shifted since the fifth century A.D."[2] In Switzerland the line that
divides the French- and German-speaking zones today is essentially the same as the line that divided the German-speaking
Alemanni from the Latin-speaking Burgundians in the fifth
century.[3]

Socioeconomic diversity, on the other hand, increases both
among and within countries with the level of socioeconomic development—with the familiar changes often called modernization, such as industrialization, urbanization, higher incomes, the
decline of the agricultural sector, and the growth of literacy and
education. These changes are intercorrelated; an increase in the
one is generally accompanied by an increase in the others. Modernization is accompanied by an enormous proliferation of specialized roles and organizations. The more affluent the country or

[2] See Val R. Lorwin, "Segmented Pluralism: Ideological Cleavage and Political
Cohesion," a paper presented to the Torino Round Table of the International Political Science Association, Sept. 1969; also Val R. Lorwin, "Belgium," in R. A. Dahl,
ed., *Political Oppositions in Western Democracies* (New Haven, 1966).

[3] Kurt Mayer, "Cultural Pluralism and Linguistic Equilibrium in Switzerland,"
in Joseph J. Spengler and Otis Dudley Duncan, eds., *Demographic Analysis* (Glencoe, Ill., 1956), pp. 481–82.

community, the more it demands specialization and the more it can afford to produce and support specialists. To put the matter much too simply, an agrarian community made up in large part of illiterate peasants dominated by a relatively simple hierarchy of status, wealth, and power develops into an urban-industrial community with a vast array of trades, occupations, professions, and roles, in intricate patterns of status, wealth, and power. Political life tends to follow a similar course of development: political roles become increasingly specialized, full-time, professional, organized.

Finally, both cultural and socioeconomic diversities appear to increase with the size of community within a given country but not among different countries. Within countries, smaller communities tend to be relatively homogeneous, larger communities relatively heterogeneous. The size of a community within a country is in turn related to its level of socioeconomic development: a small community is more likely to be oriented toward agriculture or to have a relatively simple economic structure, whereas a large city is more likely to be economically "advanced." Hence the fact that, within countries, categoric diversity increases with the size of the community might appear to be explainable entirely by the corresponding increases in socioeconomic level: the larger the community, the higher its socioeconomic level; the higher the socioeconomic level, the greater the categoric diversity in the community.

Yet this is evidently not the whole story. Higher socioeconomic levels may account for much of the growing diversity and specialization of roles and organizations.[4] But they can hardly explain greater diversity within such historic categories as language and religion, i.e. cultural diversity. Yet the evidence shows that the larger a community, the greater its cultural diversity. To take a single example, the larger cantons of Switzerland are less homogeneous than the smaller ones with respect not only to occupations but also to language and religion. The population size of the

---

[4] There is some evidence that specialization of roles and organizations may increase with population, independently of socioeconomic level. See Kaare Svalastoga, *Social Differentiation* (New York, 1965), pp. 149–50. But the evidence is by no means clear or conclusive.

canton typically explains 25 per cent of the variation in linguistic and religious diversity among Swiss cantons.

Among countries, the evidence we have does not indicate a relationship between size and categoric diversity. One study suggests that religious heterogeneity may be greater in more populous countries (although that correlation is extremely weak), but ethnic diversity shows no discernible relationship to population size.[5] The effects of unique historical factors on religious, ethnic, and linguistic diversity, and of socioeconomic development on occupational diversity, appear to be so powerful that they overwhelm any possible effects of population size.

The absence of a relation across countries between population size and cultural diversity is further confirmed in a study using an index of pluralism that combines five variables: language, race, religion, sectionalism, and a fifth variable reflecting the extent to which interests are articulated by "kinship, lineage, ethnic, regional, and religious groups." Although this index shows no association with the size of a country's population, it does show an interesting association with area. At the extremes of heterogeneity and homogeneity, territorially big and small countries, as we might expect, differ markedly. A big country is much more likely to be highly heterogeneous than a small country. Conversely, a little country is much more likely to be highly homogeneous than a big country. "Moreover in the full table there is a linear relationship between geographic size and level of pluralism: the larger the polity, the more likely it is to be pluralistic. Indeed, 87% of the variation is due to linear regression."[6] Cultural diversity is also greater in less densely populated and less highly urbanized countries. In fact, a high degree of cultural diversity is evidently most typical of relatively new countries in which the inhabitants are scattered thinly over a comparatively large territory and live at low levels of socioeconomic development.[7] To summarize:

[5] Jack Sawyer, "Dimensions of Nations: Size, Wealth, and Politics," *American Journal of Sociology*, 73 (1967), 145–72, Tables 3A, 31.

[6] Marie R. Haug, "Social and Cultural Pluralism as a Concept in Social System Analysis," *American Journal of Sociology*, 73 (1967), 294–304, at p. 300.

[7] *Ibid.*, Tables 5, 6, and 7.

Among communities of varying populations within a country, the larger the community the greater the categoric diversity with respect both to the historic cleavages of language, religion, and culture and to the kinds of socioeconomic diversity associated with modernization.

Among countries, cultural diversity depends heavily on unique historical factors. It is not related to a country's population. However, the larger a country's territory, the more likely it is to be culturally diverse.

Among countries, socioeconomic diversity is associated with the level of "modernization." But the level of modernization is independent of population.

Both among and within countries categoric diversity may increase with population size, quite independently of unique historical factors and socioeconomic level. If so, however, the effects of population size appear to be overridden by the effects of the other two factors, for we have no firm evidence to support the view that the size of a country's population is related to categoric diversity.

Organizations

As we have already suggested, the same processes that seem to generate categoric diversity may also increase the number of organizations in a society. The prevailing view has been summed up as follows:

Because literacy, urbanization, money economy, political revolution, and previously existing organizational density affect the variables leading to high motivation to found organizations and the variables increasing the chances for success of new organizational forms, they tend to increase the rate at which new organizational forms are developed. Such, at least, is the current theory, which remains at a relatively low level of verification.[8]

[8] Arthur L. Stinchcombe, "Social Structure and Organizations," in James G. March, ed., *Handbook of Organizations* (Chicago, 1965), p. 153. For an earlier statement, see David B. Truman, *The Governmental Process* (New York, 1951), pp. 52–62.

This view is supported by data like these from the United States: according to census reports, in 1850 the United States had 38,000 local churches; by 1936 the number was almost 200,000. In 1890 there were 145 different denominations; in 1936, there were 256. In 1897 the American Federation of Labor had 58 trade unions affiliated with it; by 1920 the number had stabilized at about 110. Just before the Civil War, Dun and Bradstreet listed about 200,-000 business concerns; by 1950 the number was nearly 2.7 million. Using a different reporting system, the census reported about 3 million firms in 1929 and almost 4.5 million in 1956. In 1790 there were 24 communities with a population of 2,500 or more; in 1850, 236; in 1900, 1,737; and in 1950, 4,741.[9]

An increase in the number of organizations in a country is ordinarily attributed to the set of complex, interrelated processes called modernization. But the two major dimensions of size—population and area—also appear to be important contributing factors. Whatever the structure of authority may be, whether democratic or hierarchical, the search for effective means of communication and control seems to produce a powerful tendency within any organization to break down into subunits as it grows in size. There are limits to the "span of control" that impose imperious requirements on all organizations: if an organization does not formally recognize them, its formal structure will cease to parallel its informal structure. Some degree of decentralization is required, therefore, even in organizations dominated by hierarchical authority, such as military units or political dictatorships.

These assumptions are commonplace among students of organizations. And if they are valid for public bureaucracies, business firms, military organizations, hospitals, and a variety of other organizations, they should also carry implications for political communities. Thus it is reasonable to conjecture that:

Other things being equal — particularly the socioeconomic level — the larger the population or area of a political system, the greater the number of organizations and subunits it will contain.

9 The data are from U.S. Bureau of the Census, *Historical Statistics of the United States, Colonial Times to 1957* (Washington, D.C., 1960), pp. 14, 97, 228, 570.

Because of the difficulty of defining and identifying the boundaries of an organization or of its subunits, as well as for other reasons, the available data are so meager that this is a very difficult conjecture to test. It does, however, suggest a subsidiary hypothesis:

> Other things being equal, the larger the population or area of a political system, the more governmental subunits it will contain.

Of course the *ceteris paribus* clause in this case, as in so many others, covers a multitude of qualifications, including not only the modernity of the country but the very nature of its politics. Nonetheless, some scattered evidence does lend support to the hypothesis. Once again, comparisons within countries have proved more fruitful than comparisons among countries. In a study of 51 American communities ranging in population from 50,000 to 750,000, Clark found that "the larger the number of inhabitants in the community, the more decentralized the decision-making structure."[10] At the grosser level, larger countries are somewhat more likely to have federal governments than they are to have unitary governments.[11] Naturally, a nominally federal structure in a one-party dictatorship is not the same as a federal structure in a representative democracy. Among countries with the institutions of representative democracy, federalism is more frequent when the population or area is larger; where, presumably, size impedes communication and control. And in Switzerland, the mountainous terrain provides a kind of geographical equivalent to size. Our evidence also suggests that the larger the country, the more decentralized its government, whether federal or not. Table 3.1, for example, shows rather strong negative correlations between degree of centralization and size of country in 18 representative democracies. What is perhaps most interesting in Table 3.1 is that the relationship is much stronger with *area*

[10] Terry N. Clark, "Community Structure, Decision-Making, Budget Expenditures, and Urban Renewal in 51 American Communities," *American Sociological Review*, 33 (1968), 576–93, at p. 585.

[11] Sawyer found that among 82 countries, of which 18 were federal in structure and the rest unitary, the correlation of federal structure with size of population was .34 ("Dimensions of Nations," Table 3A, p. 162).

TABLE 3.1

Governmental Centralization and Size in 18
Representative Democracies

	Correlations between relative size of central government and size of country	
Governmental aspect	Population	Area
Employment	—.49	—.83
Expenditures	—.10	—.66
Revenues	.00	—.56

NOTE: The measure of centralization used here is the relative size of central government to all governments. The representative democracies used here and elsewhere are from a list of 35 polyarchies and near polyarchies on which suitable recent data could be found. The list is in Robert A. Dahl, *Polyarchy: Participation and Opposition* (New Haven, 1971), p. 248, and the criteria of classification are described in Appendix A, p. 231ff.

than with *population*. Historically, of course, distance has imposed severe obstacles to communication.

To be sure, the barriers imposed by space on direct communication have been radically reduced by modern transportation and even more by telephone, radio, and television. Communications costs, though not independent of distance, are a fraction of what they once were. How much the decentralization in countries with large territory reflects historic costs of communication rather than present costs it is difficult to say. Yet the need for decentralization shows no signs of disappearing.

Let us suppose that on the basis of these scanty data we accept our hypothesis that, other things being equal, the larger a country, the greater the number of organizations and subunits. Would this proliferation of subunits necessarily lead to greater diversity or complexity? Almost certainly so. Even in systems like the military, where the subunits are very similar—indeed, required to be substantially identical precisely in order to reduce complexity—an increase in size seems to involve an increase in complexity, that is, in the number of variables to be taken into account and in the variations in the relations among these variables. Although it is difficult to be sure that other things are indeed equal, it seems hardly open to doubt that a military establishment of 10 million men would be more complex than one of 10,000, 100,000, or even one million. For one thing, the subunits that are intended to be equivalent and even interchangeable are never, in practice, strictly identical, but vary enough to create problems. For another, increases in size make possible, may require, and are usually accompanied by some increase in specialization, adding further variables to the system. Then, too, every organization or subunit tends to develop its own interests or goals, along with leaders and other members willing to invest time, energy, and wit to achieve them. To this extent, organizations and subunits tend to become interest groups.

Once again, this line of reasoning is familiar to students of organizations and interest groups. There is, however, an additional reason for thinking that the number of interest groups may increase with the size of a political system. Just as organization theory assumes an upper threshold of size beyond which the span of control is too great for effective communication and control, so we assume a lower threshold of size below which it is unlikely that a separate interest group will be organized. In fact, it is tempting to formulate what might be called the Plumber's Law. If there is approximately one plumber to every 1,000 people, then a community of 1,000 inhabitants is likely to have only one plumber—and no specific organization of plumbers. A town of 10,000 will have about 10 plumbers, and a better chance of a plumbers' union. A city of 100,000 will have 100 plumbers or so, and very likely an organization of plumbers. A city of a million, with 1,000 plumbers, will probably have a plumbers' organization with a number of subunits and some specialized services.

This general line of reasoning leads directly to a hypothesis that is often associated with the name of James Madison:

> The larger the size of a political system (whether size is measured by population or by area), the greater the number of organized interests or interest groups.

Unfortunately, there seems to be no satisfactory way at present to test this hypothesis. We must therefore leave it as a highly plausible conjecture.

To sum up, a great deal of theory and impression, and very little quantitative data, support the following conjectures:

Other things being equal — particularly the socioeconomic level of a country — the larger a country, the greater the number of organizations and subunits it will contain, the more governmental subunits it will contain, and the greater the number of organized interests or interest groups it will contain.

Other things being equal, among countries with representative democratic institutions, the larger the country, the more complex its policy-making processes will be.

FOUR

Citizen Participation and Sense of Effectiveness

Does the extent to which citizens participate in political life in democratic systems, where the legal opportunities to participate are comparatively extensive, depend in any significant way on the size of the system?

Theoretical Considerations

The incentive to participate in politics might be expected to increase:

a) The greater the direct satisfaction (or avoidance of dissatisfaction) a citizen expects as a more or less immediate result of participation;

b) The lower the direct costs of participation in time, inconvenience, energy, money, embarrassment, anxiety, fear, and so on;

c) The greater the net long-run benefits (or the less the net long-run losses) expected as the indirect or distant end product of participation; and

d) The greater the chance, in the citizen's view, that his action will make a significant difference in the outcome, that is, that he will be effective.

It is certainly plausible to think that the amount of direct satisfaction a citizen receives from participation in politics (and the amount of dissatisfaction avoided) would be related in some way to the size of his community. Among social scientists and novelists it is widely held that the smaller a community, where actions are more visible, violation of norms is more threatening, conflicting norms are more intolerable, and there is less categoric and cultural diversity than in larger communities, the greater will be the conformity to a set of common norms. If the obligation to participate in politics is a widespread norm in democratic countries, one might suppose that there would be more conformity to the norm in smaller communities than in larger ones. Conceivably, too, in the smaller community participation might be thought of as less private and more social and sociable. At the same time, however, the capacity of a community to enforce conformity to a prevailing norm must dissipate rapidly as the size of the community increases; it seems improbable, therefore, that the effects would be noticeable among a group of cities with populations over, say, 100,000—or among countries over some lower limit of this kind. Among countries, the proportion of the population living in small communities might explain more than the total population of the country. Thus a large country in which most of the population lived in small towns might produce much greater conformity to the norms of good citizenship—might have higher voting turnouts, for example—than a much smaller country in which most people lived in large cities.

As to direct costs, although it is reasonable to suppose that the inconvenience of *some* political actions will be greater the larger a system is—a hypothesis we shall return to in a moment—there does appear to be no reason why the costs of *voting* in elections should increase. Voting can be made easier or more difficult by increasing or decreasing the facilities for voting. In principle, a voting booth can be as near to the voter in a large country or a large city as in a small country or a small town. In fact, low densities of population would be more likely to increase the costs of voting than would large population or large territory. Yet even in low-density areas, voting could, at least in principle, be made as easy as in high-density areas if the government, parties, or other organizations were willing and able to assume the costs.

While the net long-run benefits of political participation might vary with the type of unit, there is no reason why differences in the size of a particular kind of unit, such as a country, province, or municipality, would influence expectations about benefits in any uniform way. One might readily imagine, for example, that in a smaller country citizens would tend to be aware of harsher limits on the country's autonomy, set by international economic and political factors; consequently the options available to policy makers would be more reduced; so, presumably, the importance attached to participation would be less. Yet the same assumptions could also lead to the opposite hypothesis: precisely because of the limits set by international factors, citizens might be even more concerned about choosing and influencing a government that would have the ability to extract maximum advantages and suffer minimum losses from actions on the international scene. Moreover, some functions that in a large country would be distributed to local or intermediate governments might in a very small country be concentrated in the national government; as a result, national politics might take on even more significance in a small country than in a large one. The essential point of these speculations, then, is that they lead to no firm prediction.

The effects of size on the expected effectiveness of political participation are also difficult to predict theoretically, because effectiveness appears to be a function of at least two variables on which increasing size may have opposite effects.

On the one hand, the commonsense assumption of Rousseau and many other advocates of smallness argues that as the number of citizens increases, any particular citizen's share in power, influence, or decision making necessarily declines. Thus, in a committee of five, one vote has a vastly greater chance of being decisive than in an electorate of fifty million. Considering only this effect, as many advocates do, we would hypothesize that:

> The larger the citizen body, the weaker the sense of individual effectiveness (the greater the sense of powerlessness), hence the weaker the incentive to participate, hence the less the participation.

Yet there is a factor, which Rousseau could hardly have known about, that runs in the opposite direction. Whether one's individual action (or for that matter group action) makes a significant difference in the outcome depends on how close the balance of forces is within that system. In a very close decision, the action or inaction of a single citizen could be decisive: in a hairline election, for example, one person might cast (or fail to cast) the ballot that made the difference. Hence, if the forces are closely balanced, the incentive to participate should be higher. Evidence from American elections supports this conjecture: voters who expect an election to be a tight race are more likely to turn out than voters who expect it to be a shoo-in.

Now the argument of the last chapter and evidence to be introduced in Chapter 6 indicate that the larger a political system is, the more politically competitive it is likely to be; conversely, the smaller it is, the more politically one-sided or homogeneous it is likely to be. These considerations suggest the hypothesis that:

> The greater the population of a political system, the closer the balance of forces (more competitive) a democratic system is likely to be; hence, the greater the chance that a citizen's act of participation will have an impact on the outcome.

Considering only this effect, one might expect participation to increase with the size of the system.

It seems plausible to argue from purely theoretical considerations, then, that increasing size will have diverse and contradictory effects on political participation and that many of these effects may be offset by cultural, educational, and organizational factors. Where theory leaves us completely stranded, we can be rescued only by data. Unhappily, even the data cannot, at present, take us far. However, we shall use the data available to us for comparing levels of participation in three ways: among countries, between local and national governments in single countries, and among similar local units of different sizes within single countries.

Participation and Effectiveness Among Countries: Voting

As to voting, the data confirm our guess that there is no relationship between size of unit and electoral turnout. Specifically, there seems to be no significant relationship between turnout in national elections and population, area, or density among some 33 representative democracies. Using the logarithms of population, area, and population density, produces the following correlations:

Turnout and population	0.05
Turnout and area	−0.12
Turnout and density	−0.10

Considering the interaction of the four explanatory factors introduced at the beginning of this chapter to explain participation, this finding will not be surprising. A factor that varies independently of size, for example, is the cost of voting. It is true that one large country, the United States, has made voting much more difficult than most other countries—by registration requirements, by holding elections on a working day rather than a holiday, and, until recently, in the South, by de facto exclusion of blacks. It is true that some smaller democracies, like the Netherlands, have made failure to vote costly by penalizing nonvoters. But these are hardly necessary correlates of size. Most small countries do not have compulsory voting; and when the Netherlands abandoned it recently, participation in elections dropped off sharply. Many larger countries—Italy is an example—make voting both easy and virtually compulsory, and have extraordinarily high rates of turnout in elections.

For the reasons suggested in our discussion, expected benefits and sense of effectiveness also have only a tenuous relationship with the size of a country. In voting, the nature of the election system complicates matters even further. For example, to determine his chances of making a significant impact on the outcome of a national election, a highly rational citizen would have to calculate whether his vote was likely to change the outcome both in his election district and in the country as a whole. Here we enter a realm where precise calculations break down and even well-informed citizens must operate according to very rough assumptions. It is obvious that, in a system with a small total population divided into small constituencies, the chance of a single vote's determining the outcome is greater than in a system with a large overall population divided into large constituencies. It is much less clear how a political system with a larger electorate but smaller constituencies would affect a voter's expectations as compared with a system that contained a smaller electorate but larger constituencies.

Even the effects of proportional representation versus winner-take-all systems are unclear. Winner-take-all ought to heighten incentives in close districts and weaken them in one-sided districts. Proportional representation means that votes cast for minority candidates are not necessarily wasted; but a proliferation of parties, as the organizers of Reform '66 have contended in the Netherlands, may damage the voter's sense of effectiveness because he has so little direct influence on the complex process of cabinet formation in the parliament. Reform '66 therefore advocates the replacement of the proportional representation system in the Netherlands by single-member districts.

Among Countries: Other Kinds of Participation

If participation in elections is not significantly affected by the size of a country, what about other forms of participation? After all, even though voting and elections have come to command a great deal of attention in representative democracies, in the older vision of direct democracy the act of voting would have been nothing more than the final show of hands—a culmination of discussion, persuasion, and debate both inside and outside the popular assembly, a ratification of popular preferences formed before the vote.

Because reports on voting in elections provide analysts with easily accessible quantitative data, elections have been far more thoroughly studied than other forms of political participation. Once we leave the relatively firm terrain of voting, cross-national comparisons become a quagmire of unknowns. Do citizens of small countries participate in political life (other than voting) more, or less, than citizens of larger countries? Do they feel themselves to be more effective? Are they more deeply interested and involved in politics? Questions like these are impossible to answer satisfactorily at present, both because of shortages of data and because the effects of size may be masked by more critical influences—cultural, educational, and so on. The fragmentary data available, however, support the conjecture that rates of political participation do not vary systematically with the size of a country. Thus, among the four representative democracies surveyed by Almond and Verba (the United States, Britain, West Germany, and Italy), the sample of citizens from the United States—which has a lower rate of turnout in national elections than the other three—consistently expressed more interest and activity in politics than citizens in those countries.[1] Yet many of the differences among these countries are markedly reduced if the effects of education are eliminated. It would be difficult to show, then, that the cross-national differences Almond and Verba found in the political behavior of the four countries are related to the fact that the population of the United States is about four times that of the others.

Indeed, for whatever it may be worth, Americans consistently report a higher level of interest in political affairs than the citizens of most other countries. Thus a comparison of survey evidence from France and from the United States led Converse and Dupeux to conclude that "Americans gauge their interest in their elections at a rather higher level than do the French."[2] In separate surveys done in the United States and the Netherlands during the 1950's, a larger proportion of Americans than of Dutch citizens said they were very much interested (see Table 4.1). The questions used in the two countries were not identical (see the table note), but they appear to measure about the same attitudes.

Data from the Dutch survey just referred to and from a survey of voters done in Tampere, Finland, shortly before the elections for a new parliament in 1958, enable us to compare interest in politics in two countries of which one has three times the population of the other. Although slight differences in the question and important differences in the classification of the responses somewhat vitiate the comparison, the percentage reporting that they were "very much interested" is about the same in both coun-

[1] Gabriel A. Almond and Sidney Verba, *The Civic Culture: Political Attitudes and Democracy in Five Nations* (Princeton, N.J., 1963).

[2] Philip E. Converse and Georges Dupeux, "Politicization of the Electorate in France and the United States," in Angus Campbell, Philip E. Converse, Warren E. Miller, and Donald E. Stokes, *Elections and the Political Order* (New York, 1966), p. 272.

TABLE 4.1

Interest in National Elections in the United States and the Netherlands

Response	Netherlands 1956	United States 1952
Very much interested	21%	37%
Somewhat (*tamelijk*) interested	45	34
Not interested	28	28
Not ascertained	1	1
TOTAL	100%	100%

SOURCE: Netherlands, *De Nederlandse Kiezer*, 1956, p. 73; U.S., Angus Campbell, Gerald Gurin, and Warren E. Miller, *The Voter Decides* (Evanston, Ill., 1954), p. 34.

NOTE: The actual questions were (U.S.) "Would you say that you have been very much interested, somewhat interested, or not much interested in following the political campaign this year?" and (Netherlands) "Have you been in general interested in the elections to the Second Chamber? Very much interested, somewhat interested, not interested?"

tries—and very low (Table 4.2). Table 4.3 compares membership in associations of all kinds in several countries.

As to involvement in political organizations, a comparison between France and the United States with respect to "memberships in political organizations, attendance at political rallies, and attempts to influence the political choice" reveals that despite gross disparities in population and area, the cross-national similarities are "impressive," and "the frequency of attendance by attender [is] almost indistinguishable between the two countries. The mean number of meetings attended among those who attended at all is in both cases a slight fraction over two."[3] A comparison between the United States and Norway reveals that, relatively speaking, almost six times as many Norwegians as Americans belong to a political party. Yet for overt partisan activities, such as attending political meetings or working for a party, the proportions are about the same (see Table 4.4).

Nearly three times as many Finns in Tampere were party members as Americans in the samples dealt with in Table 4.5. Thus among three countries—Norway, Finland, and the United States —party membership appears to decrease with population. That this is surely less a result of size factors than of differences in the party systems themselves—particularly the key role of the Norwegian labor movement in the Labor Party—is suggested by two

3 *Ibid.*

TABLE 4.2

Interest in Political Parties in the Netherlands and Finland (Tampere)

Response	Men		Women		All respondents	
	Netherlands	Finland	Netherlands	Finland	Netherlands	Finland
Very much interested	13%	15%	6%	4%	10%	8%
Somewhat interested	45	30	33	14	40	21
A little interested		42		57		51
Not interested	42	12	61	25	47	20
Not ascertained		1				3
TOTAL	100%	100%	100%	100%	100%	100%

SOURCE: For the Netherlands (election of 1956) see Table 4.1; for Tampere (election of 1958) see Pertti Pesonen, *An Election in Finland: Party Activities and Voter Reactions* (New Haven, 1968), p. 61.

TABLE 4.3

Organizational Membership in Five Countries

Category	Netherlands ($N = 1,600$)	United Kingdom ($N = 963$)	West Germany ($N = 955$)	Italy ($N = 995$)	United States ($N = 970$)
Nonmembers	50%	53%	56%	71%	43%
Members	50	47	44	29	57
Single memberships	32	31	32	24	25
Multiple memberships	18	16	12	6	32

SOURCE: Arend Lijphart, *The Politics of Accommodation* (Berkeley, Calif., 1968), p. 150. Adapted from Centraal Bureau voor de Statistiek, *Vrijestijdbesteding in Nederland, Winter 1955/'56*, Deel 5, *Verenigingsleven* (Zeist, 1957), p. 10; and Gabriel A. Almond and Sidney Verba, *The Civic Culture: Political Attitudes and Democracy in Five Nations* (Princeton, N.J., 1963), pp. 302, 320. In tables presenting data from these two sources (and unpublished data from the Almond and Verba survey), unless otherwise noted, the sample *N*'s for these countries will be as shown here.

things. As Table 4.4 shows, party membership does not appear to involve overt political activity; and as Table 4.5 shows, there is a somewhat higher proportion of political partisans in the United States. As Table 4.5 also shows, the proportion of strong party supporters is not systematically related to the proportion of party members in the three samples. Moreover, the proportion of strong party identifiers appears to be higher in Finland than in the United States, and almost twice as high in Finland as in Norway, whereas the proportion of nonpartisans or independents in Tam-

TABLE 4.4
*Party Membership and Electoral Activity in Norway
and the United States*

Norway (N = 2,563)		United States (N = 1,772)	
Question	Positive responses	Question	Positive responses
Are you a member of any political party?	23%	Do you belong to any political club or organization?	4%
Were you yourself present at one or more election meetings or political rallies this autumn?	8	Did you go to any political meetings, rallies, dinners, or things like that?	9
Did you yourself take an active part in the election work for any of the parties this autumn?	3	Did you give any money to help the campaign for one of the parties or candidates?	12
		Did you do any other work for one of the parties or candidates?	4

SOURCE: Stein Rokkan and Angus Campbell, "Citizen Participation in Political Life: A Comparison of Data for Norway and the United States of America," *International Social Science Journal,* 12, no. 1 (1960), 66–99.

TABLE 4.5
Political Partisanship in Norway, Finland, and the United States

Indicator and categories of partisanship	Norway (N = 2,563)	Finland (Tampere) (N = 476)	United States (N = 1,772)
Party membership	23%	11%	4%
Strong supporters (including party members)	25%	44%	36%
Weak supporters	34	39	37
Nonpartisans or independents	25	11	23
No information, other	16	6	4
TOTAL	100%	101%	100%

SOURCE: For party membership see note to Table 4.4 and (for Tampere) Pesonen, p. 66; for categories of partisanship see Angus Campbell and Henry Valen, "Party Identification in Norway and the United States," in Campbell *et al., Elections and the Political Order.*

pere seems to be less than half that in Norway or the United States. These findings are not surprising: partisanship is, obviously, a result of influences having nothing to do with size. In the case of the Finns, the presence of a strong Communist party and the lingering legacy of the Civil War may well stimulate strong party preferences.

These scattered data are a fragile foundation for generalizing, but they do lend some support to the conjecture that:

Among countries, there does not appear to be any general relationship between political participation and size. If there is a relation, it is so slight in comparison with other factors affecting participation that it cannot be detected from existing data.

Among Countries: Effectiveness

Even if political participation is not related to the size of a country, citizens of a smaller country might feel more effective in politics than citizens of larger countries. After all, one might conjecture, the mere fact that citizens could be more effective might make leaders of smaller countries so responsive that less action by citizens would actually be necessary. Whatever the validity of the conjecture—we shall return to it—it appears that:

Citizens in smaller democracies do not feel more effective than citizens in larger countries.

To begin with, a bit of data shows that something more than size is at work. Citizens in Dublin, capital of the third smallest European democracy in population, show considerably less confidence of equal treatment and serious consideration by public officials than citizens of four other, much larger countries; in fact, their pessimism is exceeded only by that of the sample of citizens in Mexico, which we do not classify as a representative democracy (see Table 4.6).

Second, survey data assembled by Arend Lijphart and Almond and Verba enable us to compare the sense of effectiveness in the Netherlands and four larger representative democracies (Table 4.7). As Lijphart points out, in the face of a potentially harmful or unjust action,[4]

53 per cent do not feel competent to do anything at all; they either do not know what they would do or explicitly state that they would do nothing. More than half of the Dutch respondents would simply resign themselves to such potentially harmful or unjust action. The percentage of passivity is considerably higher than in the United States

[4] Arend Lijphart, *The Politics of Accommodation* (Berkeley, Calif., 1968), p. 151.

TABLE 4.6

*Citizens' Expectations of Treatment by Government Officials
and the Police*

Expectation	Dublin	United States	United King-dom	West Germany	Italy	Mexico
Treatment by Public Officials						
They expect equal treatment	55%	83%	83%	65%	53%	42%
They don't expect equal treatment	35	9	7	9	13	50
They expect serious consideration for point of view	37	48	59	53	35	14
They expect a little attention	35	31	22	18	15	48
They expect to be ignored	17	6	5	5	11	27
Treatment by Police						
They expect equal treatment	75	85	89	72	56	32
They don't expect equal treatment	20	8	6	5	10	57
They expect serious consideration for point of view	62	56	74	59	35	12
They expect a little attention	23	22	13	11	13	46
They expect to be ignored	10	11	5	4	12	29

SOURCE: The body of this table is reproduced without change from Basil Chubb, *The Government and Politics of Ireland* (Stanford, Calif., 1969), p. 311. Chubb's sources were the unpublished Munger Survey (Dublin) and Almond and Verba, *Civic Culture*, pp. 108–9 (all others).

NOTE: Here and elsewhere in tables based on the Almond and Verba survey, the sample *N* for Mexico is 1,007 unless otherwise noted.

(25 per cent) and the United Kingdom (38 per cent), and not strikingly lower than in Germany (63 per cent).

If (as we shall see in a moment) citizens believe themselves to be more effective in dealing with local than with national governments, why, it might be asked, shouldn't citizens in smaller democracies like Ireland or the Netherlands feel much more effective in dealing with their officials than citizens of very much larger countries like the United States, Britain, and Germany?

First, national governments may be so different from local governments that evidence of the kind presented here could be largely irrelevant. All national governments, for example, may be so complex, or all except a few countries may be so large, that the effects of differences in size are trivial or nonexistent.

Second, political confidence, sense of competence, belief in the

TABLE 4.7
Sense of Political Effectiveness in Five Countries

Action respondents would take to prevent harmful or unjust government action	Nether- lands	United Kingdom	West Germany	Italy	United States
Try to enlist others	30%	23%	20%	10%	34%
Act alone	23	50	23	19	64
Do nothing	43	32	56	50	21
Don't know	11	6	7	22	4
TOTAL	107%	111%	106%	101%	123%

SOURCE: For the Netherlands, Lijphart, pp. 152–53; for all others, Almond and Verba, *Civic Culture*, p. 203.
NOTE: Percentages of more than 100 are due to multiple responses.

accessibility of officials, sense of personal effectiveness, and similar orientations toward government are almost certainly influenced by factors having nothing to do with size, such as the level of education in a country, the nature of its political institutions, its political culture, and its historical evolution. These influences may be—and probably are—so powerful as to override any effects size might have in cross-national comparisons. In any case, only by controlling for these factors would we be able to detect whether size of country makes any independent contribution to the citizen's sense of effectiveness.

Participation and Effectiveness: Local Versus National

Whatever the effects of size may be on participation and effectiveness, they are evidently too slight or too subtle to show up among democratic countries, at least in the gross data now available to us. Particularly because of the obscuring or nullifying impact of the kinds of cross-national differences just mentioned, it may prove more profitable to look at differences within countries. Within countries, two kinds of comparison seem useful. Within any given democratic country, we can examine variations in participation among units of essentially the same legal or constitutional form; for example, variations among municipalities of different sizes, or among states, or among provinces. We can also look for variations among units of different types and sizes, particularly local governments as compared with national. We have

TABLE 4.8
Sense of Understanding the Issues in Five Countries

Respondents' evaluation of how well they understand	United States		United Kingdom		West Germany		Italy		Mexico	
	Nat'l	Local	Nat'l	Local	Nat'l	Local	Nat'l	Local	Nat'l	Local
Very well	7%	21%	8%	18%	13%	25%	7%	15%	1%	5%
Moderately well	38	44	36	36	35	37	20	23	7	13
SUBTOTAL	45	65	44	54	48	62	27	38	8	18
Not so well	37	23	36	25	24	18	24	19	46	49
Not at all	14	10	15	14	15	7	33	27	43	31
SUBTOTAL	51	33	51	39	39	25	57	46	89	80
Depends, don't know, etc.	4	2	5	6	13	13	16	16	3	1
TOTAL	100%	100%	100%	99%	100%	100%	100%	100%	100%	99%

SOURCE: Almond and Verba, unpublished data.
NOTE: The questions were (15) "Thinking of the important national and international issues facing the country, how well do you think you can understand these issues?" and (16) "How about the local issues in this town or part of the country? How well do you understand them?" The sample N for Mexico here is 1,295.

only a very limited amount of data for comparisons of either kind, but what we have points to some interesting conclusions.

First of all, then, how do local units compare with the national level in the four factors bearing on incentives to participate that were mentioned at the beginning of this chapter: direct satisfactions, direct costs, net long-run benefits, and expected effectiveness? The evidence, though fragmentary, supports the view that at least some of these factors are more favorable to participation at the local than at the national level.

Although direct satisfactions and costs have not been satisfactorily measured, there is evidence that at least in some countries citizens tend to believe that their local government is a more human-sized institution, that what it does is more understandable, that it handles questions they can more readily grasp, and thus is more rewarding, less costly, to deal with. Great matters of foreign affairs, military policy, and national and international fiscal and monetary policy are likely to be remote and complex for a great many people (even for those reluctant to admit it). By contrast, the questions their local government deals with seem a good deal simpler. In the United States, for example, over half the respondents interviewed in the Almond and Verba survey confessed that they did not understand national issues at all, or at any rate not so very well, whereas only a third felt baffled by local issues. The number who said they understood local issues "very well" was three times as great as the number who said they understood national issues very well. Local issues were also better grasped in the other countries studied (see Table 4.8).

A survey done in Germany in 1964, with a much larger sample (2,140), produced results very similar to those shown in Table 4.8: 67 per cent of the respondents said they understood local issues either "very well" or "fairly well," whereas only 52 per cent could say the same for national isues. At the other end of the scale, 35 per cent of the respondents admitted they understood national issues either "not so well" or "not at all," whereas only 20 per cent said this of local issues.[5]

[5] *DIVO*, July 1964 ($N = 2,140$), reported in *Polls*, 1, no. 2 (Summer 1965), 25–26.

TABLE 4.9
Reported Impact of Governments on Daily Lives in Five Countries

Respondents' evaluations	United States Nat'l	United States Local	United Kingdom Nat'l	United Kingdom Local	West Germany Nat'l	West Germany Local	Italy Nat'l	Italy Local	Mexico Nat'l	Mexico Local
Degree of Impact										
Great effect	41%	35%	33%	23%	38%	33%	23%	19%	7%	6%
Some effect	44	53	40	51	32	41	31	39	23	23
No effect	11	10	23	23	17	18	19	22	66	67
Other	0	—	—	—	—	—	3	2	—	—
Don't know	4	2	4	3	12	8	24	18	3	3
TOTAL	100%	100%	100%	100%	99%	100%	100%	99%	99%	100%
Character of impact										
Tends to improve	74%	69%	73%	63%	56%	60%	50%	52%	18%	14%
Sometimes improves, sometimes not	18	23	14	18	28	26	17	15	6	7
Better off without	3	4	5	9	3	1	9	9	6	7
Other, don't know, etc.	5	4	7	9	14	13	24	23	71	72
TOTAL	100%	100%	99%	99%	101%	100%	100%	99%	101%	100%

SOURCE: Almond and Verba, *Civic Culture*, pp. 80–82; Almond and Verba survey, unpublished data.

NOTE: The questions asked regarding the character of governmental impact can be paraphrased as follows: "On the whole, do the activities of the national/local government tend to improve conditions in this area, or would one be better off without them?" Since the latter question was asked only of those who attributed some impact to government, the N's for this question are correspondingly reduced. For national governments, for example, they are as follows: U.S. 821, U.K. 707, W. Germany 676, Italy 534, and Mexico 301.

As to benefits, citizens in democratic countries do not seem to look upon their local governments as markedly less important in their daily lives than the national government. For example, although in each of the five countries surveyed by Almond and Verba, the national government was more frequently said to have great effect on daily life than the local governments, the differences were not great (see Table 4.9). Nearly as many citizens in each of these countries said that the activities of local government tended to improve conditions in the area as said this about national governments; almost none felt that they would be better off without local government.

As to effectiveness, in the five-nation survey, citizens saw local units as more accessible, more subject to their control, more manageable. In the United States, only one citizen in ten thought he would stand much chance of success in changing a proposed national law he considered unjust; but more than one out of four thought they could succeed in changing a proposed local regulation they considered unjust. In all five countries, in fact, the proportion of citizens who felt they could change a proposed national law they felt unjust or harmful was lower than the proportion who felt they could change an unjust local regulation. A survey of voters in Amsterdam in 1966 revealed that about two out of three felt that they had no influence on politics. But slightly fewer (63 per cent as opposed to 69 per cent) were pessimistic about their influence on local as opposed to national politics (see Table 4.10).[6]

All these findings naturally lead one to expect that citizens participate more in local politics than in national politics. Yet we immediately encounter the following paradox:

> In a number of countries, including the United States, levels of political participation other than voting are higher at local than at national levels; but voter turnout is lower.

The evidence for participation other than voting again comes from the Almond and Verba survey of five countries. To be sure,

[6] *Acta Politica*, 1967, p. 110. $N = 1,513$.

TABLE 4.10
Sense of Political Effectiveness at National and Local Levels in Five Countries

Estimated likelihood of changing unjust or harmful law	United States		United Kingdom		West Germany		Italy		Mexico	
	Nat'l	Local	Nat'l	Local	Nat'l	Local	Nat'l	Local	Nat'l	Local
Very likely, moderately likely	11%	28%	12%	19%	7%	23%	8%	19%	29%	37%
Somewhat unlikely	18	15	18	22	25	27	13	20	11	10
Not at all likely, impossible	36	25	44	28	48	22	50	32	50	44
Likely only if others joined in	24	25	12	17	6	9	3	3	—	—
Other, don't know	9	6	13	14	14	18	26	27	10	9
TOTAL	100%	100%	99%	100%	100%	99%	100%	101%	100%	100%

SOURCE: Almond and Verba survey, unpublished data.

NOTE: The questions were, "Suppose a regulation were being considered by (22, 23) the most local government unit: town, village, etc., or (26, 27) a law by the national legislature that you considered very unjust or harmful . . . , what could you do (22, 26)? If you made an effort to change this regulation (law), how likely is it that you would succeed (22, 27)?"

TABLE 4.11

Reported Attempts to Influence the Government in Five Countries

Country	National government	Local government
United States	16%	28%
United Kingdom	6	15
West Germany	3	14
Italy	2	8
Mexico	3	6

SOURCE: Almond and Verba survey, unpublished data.
NOTE: The N for Mexico here is 1,295.

in every one of the five, it is only a minority of citizens who ever try to influence governments except by voting. But within those minorities, some two to four times as many people said they had tried to influence their local government as said they had tried to influence their national government (Table 4.11). A survey in the Netherlands in 1956 showed similar results: six times as many people (12 per cent) reported having contacted a municipal councilor as reported having contacted a member of parliament (2 per cent).[7]

Over against this we must place the finding that within countries

> There is a general tendency for turnout in national elections to be higher than in local elections, even though in some countries the differences are quite small.

To explain the paradox we need to make a distinction between the impact of a particular level of government and the perceived consequences of elections. Citizens may feel that a local government has an important impact without having so strong a desire to participate in a local election as in a national election. For one thing, given that in most countries local elections are more lopsided than national elections (we return to this point in a later chapter), incentives to participate are reduced. Quite naturally, national elites regard national elections as more important than local elections. As a consequence they focus more attention on the national election; the mass media

---

[7] *De Nederlandse Kiezer*, 1966, p. 73.

devote far more attention to it; organizations work harder to activate their supporters. When this is not the case, as in Italy and Chile, where municipal or provincial elections are held throughout the country on the same day and where the elections are viewed as interim referendums and shifts in partisan percentages are interpreted as trends in national support, the falloff in turnouts is very much less than in countries like the United States and Britain, where local elections are much more insulated from national political life.

Thus the discrepancy in turnouts ought not to be interpreted as meaning that participation in local political life is, for most people, necessarily less significant or satisfying than participation in national politics. The political elites, who may often see local politics as an early step in the *cursus honorum* leading to the highest national offices, are not in this respect representative of most citizens. The fact is, as we have said, that in all democratic countries most citizens participate only marginally in political life, whether national or local. The relative immediacy, accessibility, and comprehensibility of local politics may provide many citizens with a greater sense of competence and effectiveness than they feel in the remoter reaches of national politics. What defenders of local government have contended throughout an epoch of growing centralization and nationalization of political life may prove to be more, not less, valid in the future: the virtues of democratic citizenship are, at least for the ordinary citizen, best cultivated in the smaller, more familiar habitat of local governments.

If, and as, more democratic countries become integrated into larger regional and international systems, the autonomy of the national government will of course decline. National governments may then become rather like state or local governments today; yet they will lack the advantages of proximity and familiarity. As we argued in Chapter 1, in a series of interlocking levels of government in which the nation-state loses its autonomy, it may also lose much of the claim that national elites in democratic countries have made for it during the past century— that, given the impossibility of the city-state, the nation-state has become the unique locus of "democracy." For, as we shall suggest, there will be no unique locus; much of what remains of the democratic aspirations for effective citizen participation will then have to be fulfilled in the smaller rather than the larger arenas. Among these smaller arenas, local territorial governments will probably take on renewed significance.

Participation and the Size of Local Units

Is there, then, a size or a range of sizes for local governments that is optimal for citizen participation and effectiveness? Clearly, if there is an optimal size, then much more attention should be given in the future to achieving and maintaining that size in local units.

Three points must be made at once. First, what is optimal according to one criterion—in this case participation and sense of effectiveness—may not be optimal according to other criteria. This point is of fundamental importance, and we shall return to it in the last chapter; for in our view it requires a shift in perspectives on democracy comparable in magnitude to the shift in locus from city-state to nation-state. Second, what is optimal at one time or place may not be optimal in another. This point, too, raises such basic questions that we shall have to return to it more than once. Finally, there exists a lamentable paucity of evidence on the matter. Here again, voting is of course the easiest to record and report. Voting data show that:

> Within countries, among local units of the same legal type, there is no general relationship between turnout and unit size. Thus in some democratic systems, election turnouts are somewhat higher in smaller than in larger municipalities. In others, it is the reverse. In still others, there appears to be no relationship between size and turnout.

For reasons that we have already suggested, voting is not necessarily the best—and certainly is not the only appropriate—indicator of participation and sense of effectiveness. Yet with the exception of a highly important Swedish study, which we shall turn to in a moment, data bearing on the relation between participation (other than voting) and size of local government unit are all but nonexistent.

A reanalysis of data from the American sample used in the Almond and Verba survey cited earlier has shown that among respondents in that sample, participation was not related to community size.[8] However, the sense of political powerlessness increased slightly with the size of the respondent's community. Although the presence of a larger proportion of educated people in larger communities tended to mask the relationship, with education controlled the correlation increased, "indicating that within educational levels, there is a weak but significant positive relationship between community size and feelings of political powerlessness."[9] Large urban concentrations apparently do contribute to a sense of estrangement between the citizen and his government. Although the correlation of powerlessness with size was lower than with education and age, it was higher than the correlations with sex, income, and race.[10] It seems anomalous that although a sense of political powerlessness increases with the size of the community, participation does not decline. Again the explanation may be that the effects on participation were masked by the fact that respondents from the larger communities tended to have had more education—and thus, as we know from a multitude of other studies, would be more likely to participate in politics.

The Swedish Study

The largest and most careful study bearing on the relation of size to democracy within a country is the work of the Local Government Research Group in Sweden.[11] The group chose 36 local

8 Ada W. Finifter, "Dimensions of Political Alienation," *American Political Science Review*, 64 (1970), 389–410. The index of political participation was constructed from seven items, e.g. "Have you ever done anything to try to influence a local decision?" "... an act of Congress?" The absence of a correlation between size of community and this index of participation is shown in Table 4, p. 398, Variables 1 and 23.

9 *Ibid.*, p. 403.

10 *Ibid.*

11 Operating under the aegis of the political science departments of the five Swedish universities, the group received a total of about one million dollars from the Tri-Centennial Fund of the Bank of Sweden. Full-scale work began in 1966

government units (communes) as the basic units of analysis; the 36 communes are a sample carefully constructed to discover the effects of varying size and density of population on democratic values and efficiency of performance.[12] Some comparisons include the three largest cities of Sweden—Stockholm with 800,000 people, Göteborg with 450,000, and Malmö with 260,000. The very small population of most Swedish communes, particularly striking, perhaps, to observers from the United States, makes this study unusually valuable in that it shows consequences of varying size persisting far below the thresholds often assumed to be significant.

The major finding of the study is that in Sweden the values of *participation and effectiveness are best achieved in densely populated communes with populations under 8,000.* For example, in these small, densely populated communes *a larger percentage of voters report that they often discuss local problems.* An explanation can be found in two factors that are associated with higher levels of discussion in all communes: membership in organizations and acquaintance with local representatives. In both respects, the smaller communes have the advantage: member-

under the chairmanship of Jörgen Westerståhl of the University of Gothenburg. Results, which are projected to fill ten volumes, have already begun to appear in Swedish. Descriptions of the study and some of its findings appear in Jörgen Westerståhl, "Decision-making Systems in 36 Swedish Communes, A Research Report," a paper prepared for delivery at the 1970 Annual Meeting of the American Political Science Association; Westerståhl, "Report on Citizen Participation and Local Government in Sweden," n.d.; Westerståhl, "The Communal Research Program in Sweden," *The New Atlantis*, no. 2 (Winter 1970); and Bengt Owe Birgersson, "Municipal Politics in the Swedish Press," *Scandinavian Political Studies*, 2 (1968), 186–217. In addition, in the summer of 1971 Professor Westerståhl and other members of the research group very generously supplied us with tables and interpretations from the study. We should like to express here our deep appreciation to the Research Group for making available to us findings from their work.

12 The main sample of 36 communes excludes communes that are part of the three metropolitan areas (Stockholm, Göteborg, and Malmö) or were affected by communal mergers in 1967. After these exclusions, six communes were drawn from six of the cells of the following tabulation; figures in parentheses show the total number of communes in each cell.

Proportion of inhabitants in densely populated areas	Size of population		
	Under 8,000	8,000–30,000	Over 30,000
90–100%	6 (36)	6 (42)	6 (17)
30–90%	6 (332)	6 (50)	– (1)
0–30%	6 (305)	– (2)	–

TABLE 4.12

*Correlation of Political Awareness with Population Size
and Density in Swedish Communes*

Awareness indicator and density of population	Population of commune			Three largest cities
	Under 8,000	8,000–30,000	Over 30,000	
Could name at least one local candidate (median per cent):				
High	73.0%	62.3%	49.0%	—
Mixed	64.5%	68.5%	—	
Low	62.4%	—	—	
Could *not* name even one local official (median per cent):				
High	25.8%	35.9%	47.6%	54.0%
Mixed	34.0%	29.7%	—	
Low	36.4%	—	—	
Both knew and had attitude toward at least one local official (median per cent):				
High	54.0%	44.7%	36.0%	28.5%
Mixed	54.2%	54.2%	—	
Low	47.2%	—	—	

SOURCE: Bengt Owe Birgersson, Harry Forsell, Torsten Odmark, Lars Strömberg, and Claes Örtendahl, *Medborgarna Infromeras: Den Kommunala Självstyrelsen 2* (Stockholm, 1971), p. 205.
NOTE: The three largest cities are Stockholm, Göteborg, and Malmö.

ship in political and other voluntary organizations tends to be greatest in the small communes,[13] and the proportion of the population directly involved in local government is significantly greater in small communes than in large ones.

In the small, densely populated communes, the citizens are also better informed about politics. More of them can name at least one political candidate in the most recent local elections (see Table 4.12). Conversely, the percentage who could not name at least one local official is markedly lower. Nor is it merely a matter of knowing a name. Citizens in the smaller communes much more frequently both know officials' names and have attitudes toward them. Here the comparison with the three largest cities is quite striking.

The study also provides evidence that elected officials in the smaller, more densely populated communes are more representative of the characteristics and attitudes of their constituents.

[13] Westerståhl, "Decision-making Systems ...," p. 13.

However, we defer our discussion of these findings until the next chapter, where we turn our attention to problems of popular control over officials.

Summary

The argument of this chapter seems to us to point to the following conclusions:

1. Political participation and sense of effectiveness among citizens do not depend to any significant degree on the size of a country.

2. The effects of unit size on participation and effectiveness are, however, important within countries.

3. By virtue of their greater accessibility and understandability, local governments nurture participation and heighten the citizen's sense of effectiveness. In this respect, one of the traditional defenses of local governments seems to be supported by the evidence.

4. However, maximizing the values of participation and sense of effectiveness may require units very much smaller than is usually assumed: in Sweden, units with less than 10,000 people.

5. Thus a unit that would be optimal with respect to the values of participation and effectiveness may not be optimal with respect to the other values, such as the capacity of the unit to handle the problems of great concern to most citizens.

The last point anticipates an argument we shall return to later on.

FIVE

Citizen Communication and Control

That citizens should participate actively in politics is no doubt a necessary condition for citizen effectiveness and thus for achieving the first criterion of democracy suggested in Chapter 2. But clearly neither mere participation nor even a strong sense of effectiveness is sufficient.[1] Citizens cannot be effective unless their participation enables them to communicate their public policies and attitudes accurately to all those who influence decisions, and unless decision makers respond favorably to these communications. In this chapter we deal with the bearing of size on the capacity of citizens to communicate their policies to decision makers, and in the next with its bearing on the incentives for decision makers to respond favorably.

Consequences of Size for Communication Costs

If the number of people who determine the outcome of a decision is a function of the number of citizens in a political system —a majority, for example—and if the cost of communicating with a single decision maker remains constant, then obviously the total cost to a citizen wishing to communicate his views to each of these decision makers must increase with the number of citizens in the system. Although the point is intuitively obvious, an example may help our discussion. Suppose that the cost of trying to reach citizens in a particular system in order to try to

[1] We shall not, of course, investigate all the conditions that may be necessary and sufficient for meeting the two criteria, since in this book we are concerned only with conditions that seem to be significantly related to size.

persuade them to vote for a particular party is estimated very modestly at $1 a person. Then to reach 10 per cent of the citizen body would cost a political actor $10 if the system had 100 citizens, but $100 if the population increased to 1,000 citizens, etc.

Within a single system with a growing population, for any actor whose resources increased at least as fast as the number of citizens, the fact that costs of persuasion increase with size would create no problems. Thus if we assume, to simplify matters, that resources per capita are constant and equally distributed, then a political party whose membership increased with the population so as to remain constant at, say, 25 per cent of the citizen body could spend the same amount per person for persuasion no matter what the size of the citizen body. But the situation is more difficult for any actor whose resources do not increase as fast as the number of citizens: for example, for a party whose membership remains constant or grows more slowly than the number of citizens. For the average person, the problem is formidable, for if his resources remain more or less constant, the number of persons he can hope to persuade remains constant. Since this number is an ever smaller proportion of the citizen body, his effectiveness diminishes. Thus a citizen who has enough resources in time and money to present his case to 50 people might be highly effective in a community of 500 that is split into two groups with about 45 per cent of the voters each, with 10 per cent undecided; for he could quite possibly not only identify but reach the entire undecided group. But with a similar situation in a community of 5,000, he could reach only one per cent of the people; and in a community of 50,000, only one-tenth of one per cent. Moreover, in this last community it would be far more difficult to identify the undecided 10 per cent.

Our simple assumptions surely underestimate some of the difficulties of the individual, or any group of fixed size, in maintaining its capacity for persuasion in the face of increasing population; for many of the per capita costs of communication will increase with population size, at least above some lower threshold. What can be done in an evening meeting at the schoolhouse in a community of 1,000 will require mass printings, mass mailings, radio and television coverage, and enormous specialized bureaucracies in a community of 10 million.

Thus it seems clear that:

> Among different political systems at approximately the same level of socioeconomic development and GNP per capita, for the individual or for any group of constant size, the costs of attempting to persuade other citizens will be larger, the larger the number of citizens.

> To this extent, the larger the system, the greater the costs of participation for the citizen.

Time as a Cost in Communication: The Axiomatics of Participation

We have been expressing the costs of communication mainly in monetary terms. But one form of communication cost can be expressed more precisely in terms of time. Communication takes time. Because of this, fundamental and probably irreducible constraints on communication are imposed by the number of participants in a political system.

It is obvious that the maximum number of potential participants (Np) in a collective decision is fixed by two parameters: the amount of time available for the decision-making process (T) and the average length of time available to each participant (Tp). Thus,

Axiom 1: $Np = T/Tp$.

For example, suppose that a decision has to be made by the end of three days, of which eight hours a day, or a total of 24 hours, may be set aside for discussion and other forms of participation. If the average participant requires one hour, then the maximum number of potential participants is 24.

Now the average time available to each participant (Tp) is a product of the average time required for a participatory act (Ta) and the average number of acts for each participant (Ap). That is,

Axiom 2: $Tp = (Ta)(Ap)$.

It is also clear that:

Axiom 3: If the amount of time available (T) is fixed, then the number of potential participants (Np) can be increased only by reducing the time available to each participant (Tp).

Axiom 4: If the time available to each participant (Tp) is fixed, then the maximum number of potential participants (Np) can be increased only by increasing the total time available (T).

Axiom 5: If the total decision-making time (T) is fixed, then any increase in the average time allotted for a participatory act (Ta) requires a corresponding decrease in the number of acts for each participant (Ap), and vice versa.

A series of pencil-and-paper exercises would quickly give the reader a concrete sense of the meaning of these constraints, and we urge him to play about with these simple relationships for a few moments. We have already suggested an example of Axiom 3, where the amount of time available is fixed at 24 hours. To increase the number of potential participants from 24 to 100, we should have to reduce the time available to each participant (Tp) to about 15 minutes. If there were 1,500 participants, each could be allotted only one minute—about time enough to mark a simple ballot.

Or consider an example of Axiom 4, where the time available to each participant (Tp) is fixed. In the Assembly of all male citizens at Athens, a quorum was 6,000. Now the Athenian Glaucon, who has boundless enthusiasm for participatory democracy, proposes that no major decision, not even a declaration of war —nay, most of all, a declaration of war!—should be taken in the Assembly until every citizen present has a chance to speak for 15 minutes. Glaucon's proposal seems reasonable enough. Except that the Athenians soon discover that even if no more than a bare quorum of citizens is present, in order to make a single important decision they must attend the assembly 10 hours a day for 150 days.

Our examples so far have assumed only one intervention by each participant. But it is as obvious to Glaucon as it is to us that a single intervention scarcely follows the dialectical process of a search for truth. Full discussion in the Assembly, Glaucon argues, requires that each citizen not only speak once for or against the main proposal. He should also reply to the speeches other citizens make on the main proposal. Fines will be levied on shirkers who do not live up to their democratic obligations to participate in the discussion.

It is obvious to some of Glaucon's fellow citizens that he is either simpleminded or mad. For if each citizen speaks once on the main issue, and his speech is then followed by a rejoinder from every other citizen, the number of speeches by each participant must increase as the square of the number of participants. Glaucon's critics will point out that if the average time required for a speech were 15 minutes, if the bare quorum of 6,000 citizens were present, and if sessions were held 10 hours a day for 300 days a year, then Glaucon's rule would require the Assembly to meet for 3,000 years to reach a single decision.

Our axiomatics have enabled us, at the very least, to push an example or two to the point of utter absurdity. The essential point, however, is not at all absurd, even though it is painfully obvious: the number of people who can participate directly in a decision by speaking so as to be heard by all the other direct participants is extremely small. How small? Whether the limit is 5, 10, or 25 is not decisive. The extreme limit can hardly be much beyond 25–30, and is surely well below 50; readers with extensive committee experience would probably put the limit closer to 5 or 10. Let us then sum up the main theoretical proposition indicated by our axiomatics:

Axiom 6: The number of people who can participate in a decision by speaking directly to all the other participants rarely if ever exceeds the size of a "small group" or a typical "working" committee, that is, 25–30 persons.

Yet all the democratic systems we are concerned with here are very much bigger than a working committee. What happens to democratic systems, then, when they go beyond this range?

Axiom 7: Whenever a democratic system is larger than a working committee, leaders emerge who participate much more fully in political decisions than the average citizen.

This is inevitable. The more difficult it becomes for every citizen to participate fully, the more necessary it is that some citizens participate a great deal, and thus inevitably more than others. Indeed, experiments have shown striking differences in levels of participation even in very small groups. Here is a summary of such findings:[2]

Not only does the average amount of participation per member diminish as group size is increased, but the distribution of participation also varies. . . . Generally, in discussion groups of sizes three to eight, all members address some remarks to the group as a whole, but typically only one member, the top participator, addresses more to the group as a whole than to specific other members. As group size increases, a larger and larger proportion of the participators have total amounts of participation under their "equal" share, that is, under the mean for the group. At the same time, at least where a participating leader is appointed, the gap between the top participator and the others tends to grow proportionately greater as size increases. When the designated leader of a group is excluded, the gradient of total acts initiated by the remainder of the members tends to follow a simple curve that flattens as the size of the group increases.

From a democratic perspective, the problem is not so much that leaders appear—though the emergence of leaders surely creates problems—but that the leaders are likely to be unrepresentative. In the absence of any systematic device for ensuring representation of all points of view, how can a collection of people possibly avoid unrepresentativeness in leadership as the number of citizens grows larger? Consider what Bertrand de Jouvenel has superbly analyzed as the chairman's problem. As the number of citizens in an assembly increases, the problem of the chairman becomes more severe. He cannot possibly give everyone the floor; hence he must pick and choose. If he is a fair-minded chairman, he may try to select speakers according to

[2] A. Paul Hare, *Handbook of Small Group Research* (New York, 1962), p. 231. But see also Edwin J. Thomas and Clinton F. Fink, "Effects of Group Size," in A. P. Hare, E. F. Borgatta, and R. F. Bales, eds., *Small Groups* (New York, 1965), pp. 525–36.

their ability and the degree to which they represent a hitherto unrepresented point of view. To avoid confusion, perhaps an agenda must be prepared. If the issues on the agenda are complex, additional information will be needed. To focus debate, a recommended policy may be desirable. Who is to set the agenda, gather the needed information, and make the initial recommendations? How are these citizens chosen?[3]

We must not forget that the Assembly was not by any means the only political institution of Athens. Among others, there was also the Council of Five Hundred, chosen by lot, 50 citizens from each of the 10 tribes, to administer the daily business of the city and to prepare the agenda for the Assembly. Moreover, a well-known speaker, a leading figure, was more likely to speak at the Assembly than an ordinary citizen. Thus, de facto, Athens had a kind of representative government. We may imagine that if some citizens felt the selection of speakers was likely to be unfair, or in some way harmful to their cause, they would begin to caucus in advance in order to choose a "representative" to speak for them so that the best possible case would be made for their point of view. Hence

> *Axiom 8:* To the extent that formal or informal representative institutions do not develop, then the larger the political system, the less representative of the views of citizens the leaders are likely to be.

If we think for a moment about Glaucon's problem and the chairman's problem, and the more general problem of time, it is obvious that these problems exist only because the kinds of participation we have been concerned with require sequential communication among all decision makers. After all, two speakers at an assembly cannot both be heard by everyone if they try to speak simultaneously. The situation would be very different for forms of participation that did not have to be carried on sequentially among all decision makers, but could be carried on either simultaneously or else among only a small subset of deci-

---

[3] Cf. Bertrand de Jouvenel, "The Chairman's Problem," *American Political Science Review,* 55 (1961), 368–72.

sion makers—or even simultaneously among different subsets of decision makers.

Axiom 9: The larger the number of participants in a democratic system, the more necessary that participation take forms that do not require sequential communications among all the decision makers.

Fortunately, some important forms of individual participation—involving communication—do not require sequential communication because they can be performed more or less simultaneously. One of these is voting. Although voting is sometimes sequential in small groups (for example, among justices of the United States Supreme Court, the council of elders of the Barotse tribe in Africa, or United States Congressmen on a roll-call vote), voting can always be done more or less simultaneously; thus time imposes no significant contraints on the number of voters in a system.

Axiom 10: The costs of time need not affect the number of citizens who participate in politics by voting in elections.

But is this not also true for reading newspapers, listening to the radio, watching television, thinking about politics, forming views and attitudes, and other types of "psychological" participation? If so, then:

Axiom 11: The costs of time do not affect the number of citizens who participate in individual, "private," or "psychological" forms of political participation.

Our axiomatics lead us back directly, of course, to that great discovery by democratic theory and practice in the eighteenth century: the possibility of vastly enlarging the size of democratic units—in the historical case, from city-states to nation-states—by providing for elections in which citizens would choose representatives to whom they would delegate law-making authority. To the extent that the citizen body is divided into constituencies and citizens concentrate their communications within a few constituencies or even a single constituency, then of course communication costs in time, money, or other resources are reduced by the introduction of representation. But as the number of citizens in a representative democracy increases, new problems of communication arise. Some of these stem from the need of citizens, if they are to be effective in a representative democracy, to persuade officials.

If officials are to be responsive to the wants of citizens (or groups of citizens), they have to know what citizens (or groups) want. If officials are to know what citizens want, there must be some communication of wants from citizens to officials. If citizens are to be capable of opposing and removing officials who are not responsive, citizens have to know how officials respond. Hence there must be some communication to citizens of officials' response.

We can simplify our theorizing further by considering, initially, only those officials whose constituency is the entire system. No great confusion need arise if we call these simply the top officials, a label that will help us later on when we wish to speak of subofficials or subleaders of more limited scope or constituency, as of course we must.

> *Axiom 12:* The amount of direct communication from citizens to top officials is a function of (*a*) the number of citizens in the constituency, (*b*) the length of the average "message" from a citizen, (*c*) and the number of times the average citizen repeats his message.

Now assume still another useful (if artificial) simplification: that the citizen repeats his message only a fixed number of times— say once—to any given top official. Finally, may we deliberately proceed to the limits of absurdity by assuming (briefly) that a citizen with a message repeats it once, separately, to each top official?

One characteristic of communication between citizens and leaders is its lack of symmetry. A leader receives a large number of individual messages from citizens, but he can sometimes respond with a single message to all of them. Even in the Assembly of Athens, it was easier for Pericles to speak to all the citizens than for all the citizens to speak to Pericles. The development of modern and particularly electronic means of communication has vastly enlarged the number of citizens to whom a Pericles can speak; indeed, there is no longer any theoretical limit to the size of Pericles' audience. Yet the number who could communicate directly with a Pericles today is no larger than it was in fifth-century Athens.

> *Axiom 13:* The number of people who can communicate directly with a single leader remains more or less fixed, whereas the number of people with whom a leader can communicate directly by radio and television has no theoretical limit. This relation of leader to audience we call *asymmetrical communication.*

Solutions

One obvious solution to the communications overload is for leaders to respond by communicating to entire audiences. Though individual citizens continue to direct their messages to the decision maker, since he can no longer respond individually to each citizen he treats them collectively, as a single audience.

> *Solution A:* Top officials can deal with the communication problem created by an increasing number of citizens by asymmetrical communication, in which citizens are treated as an audience.

However, although asymmetry helps to reduce the time spent by the top official in responding directly to constituents, it does not reduce the time he spends receiving communications directly from constituents. Hence, as the volume increases, another solution must be found.

> *Solution B:* In order to encompass the increasing amount of time spent in direct communication with constituents— particularly in receiving direct communications—the calling of political leader becomes increasingly full-time.

With increasing size, then, the part-time amateur is replaced in the representatives' ranks by the full-time professional. Consider the parliamentary politician. Although it is empirically difficult to disentangle the influence of size on the professionalization of the parliamentary member from all the other factors that have been pressing in the same direction for the past century, size can hardly be dismissed. In most democratic countries, constituency size has been increased by both the extension of the franchise and steady population growth. In every country where constituencies have swelled, legislators have had to devote more and more time to politics. Is it surprising that the life of an American Congressman is so highly professionalized, considering that each member of the lower house has, on the average, 400,000 people in his district? Or that he is much more the full-time politician than the average Icelandic M.P., who has about 5,000 constituents? Contemplate the fact that in the United States the average representative has a constituency twice the entire population of Iceland or Luxembourg. Or that in 1960 the median state population in the United States was about 2.5 million, which means that even then, half the United States Senators represented states with populations about as large as the population of Ireland. Can we not imagine how the life of the Irish M.P. would be transformed were his present constituency to become the size of his whole country?

Yet professionalization has its limits as a solution to the problem of democratic communication. Once an individual becomes a full-time professional politician, he has stretched to the limit the time available to him for the pursuit of politics. From then on he must meet demands in other ways.

> *Solution C:* If the number of citizens increases while the size of the average message remains the same, the burden on each top official can be reduced by specialization.

Specialization removes the artificial constraint we laid down a moment ago: that the citizen repeat his message to each top official. At the limit, full specialization would mean that he need only communicate his message to one top official. Because the gains from this solution are so obvious, is one of the oftenest applied. Officials frequently specialize by subject matter, and citizens communicate with different officials on different subjects. An equally familiar form of specialization, common in legislatures, is specialization by territory. This is what parliamentary constituencies typically do: they make it easier for a citizen to communicate with one member or a few members from the area in which he lives.

Yet as a way of economizing on communication, specialization also has a limit. The limit is reached when every message directed by a citizen to the top officials is directed to only one of them. If at this point there is still a communcations overload, and if all the officials are already full-time at their tasks, then something else has to give.

Solution D: If the number of citizens increases, the size of the average message remains the same, and each message is communicated only to one leader, then the burden on each top official can be reduced by increasing the number of top officials.

This is, initially, an easy way out for legislatures. That it is a very common one is shown by the fact that, throughout the world, the number of legislators in the parliament is a function of the population. But this solution, too, has its limits, for legislatures are thought to be unwieldy if they become too large. In a sense, Solutions C and D both entail a loss of directness in communication. The citizen communicates with one top official, who in turn communicates with other top officials. Thus we have already moved part way toward a further solution:

Solution E: The burden of communication between citizens and top officials can be reduced by substituting indirect for direct chains of communication.

The full-time staffs of Senators and Representatives in the United States Congress are examples of indirect chains of communication. The Representative cannot possibly deal personally with all his constituents, so he develops a staff to handle many of these relationships. In a small way, the office of the Congressman is bureaucratized. The growth of a bureaucracy or administrative hierarchy is the most typical application of Solution D, a solution most visible in the executives of modern governments. (Bureaucracies, of course, have other functions, and other origins.)

What is accomplished by substituting indirect for direct chains of communication? Two things, it seems:

> *Solution E.1:* The subleaders in indirect chains of communication can reduce the burden of communication on top officials by summarizing or condensing communication.

A striking example of a condensed communication is the systematic opinion survey. An opinion poll can give a leader information about wants expressed by his constituents that he could never achieve by his own direct discussions, simply for want of time. Yet summarizing and condensation inevitably screen out some information. Interpretation enters: what is valuable information to one man is background noise to another. What March and Simon have called "uncertainty absorption" converts uncertainties into finalities. Conscious or unconscious, well-meaning or malignant and self-serving distortions may occur.

It is difficult, however, to assess precisely the loss of relevant information about wants that occurs with increasing size and increasing indirectness of communication, since so many other factors enter in. For example, the development of surveys and social research may conceivably provide information about wants that was hitherto unavailable even in a small system. However, the authority to summarize or condense information potentially and perhaps inevitably entails other authority and power. Whatever the original intentions, subleaders given such authority are unlikely to remain inert transmitters of information between citizens and top leaders. In democratic systems, citizens and top leaders may both conclude that they have much to gain from a system in which there are autonomous or quasi-autonomous subleaders with authority to respond to some wants expressed by some citizens.

> *Solution E.2:* Subleaders can reduce the burden of communication between citizens and top officials by acting autonomously: that is, by making decisions themselves.

In some systems, subleaders may be expressly granted the authority to make decisions. Typically, their authority will be specialized by subject matter, or territory, or both. In democratic countries, for example, virtually all elected legislatures have some kind of committee system, though the amount of autonomy enjoyed by the committees varies enormously. Committees thus become another link in the chain of indirect communication between citizens and top officials. De facto federalism is probably inherent in large, and certainly in giant, representative democracies. It is difficult to imagine, for example, how the European Common Market or the United States could maintain the institutions of representative democracy without territorial decentralization of authority.

Thus a central theme recurs. In order to fulfill the two criteria of democracy set out in Chapter 2, historical shifts occur in what are seen as the appropriate units and institutions for the realization of democratic goals. First there was the shift from primary democracy in the city-state to representative democracy in the nation-state. Now the locus of democracy is shifting from the nation-state to a multiplicity of interrelated units, some below, some above, and some at the level of the nation-state. It seems fair to say that democratic theory has not yet received the restatement it needs in order to provide adequate guidance in this new and complex institutional setting.

Exploring Some Hypotheses

Despite the fact that plausible and obvious propositions frequently turn out to be wrong, it would seem otiose to try here to test directly the main propositions just advanced. That is why we have called them axioms and solutions rather than hypotheses.

Nonetheless, the argument suggests some hypotheses worth exploring, even with the limited amount of relevant data available to us. For example, as we saw in the last chapter, voting turnout is not consistently related to size among democratic countries. This of course is what our theory of communication costs would predict and what it explains. At the same time, we would expect many other forms of participation to become more difficult as increasing population size increased communication costs, particularly time-related costs.

In addition, if, as seems reasonable, the citizen's sense of effectiveness decreases as communication costs increase, our theory would lead us to expect citizens to feel less effective in their dealings with national than with local governments, and in dealing with larger than with smaller local governments within a country. And, as we saw in the last chapter, the evidence does support this expectation. However, the theory would also predict that citizens of smaller countries would feel more effective in dealing with their national government than would citizens of larger countries. Yet we found no support for this prediction in the extremely limited data. The absence of any apparent relationship might be explained, we suggested, by the particular political culture involved, and specifically by practices that are independent of size and much more powerful in their effects. Size may have some impact at the level of the nation-state, but it is at present undetectable.

Size and Legislative Representation

A larger citizen population could be accommodated under Solution D by a proportionate increase in the number of top elected officials. As we suggested, however, this solution has definite limits. As the membership of a parliament increases, all the factors expressed in our axioms come into play. Discussion becomes more burdensome; participation in debate must be more and more severely restricted; delegation of authority to committees creates problems of coordination and collective control. The parliament, in short, becomes less and less capable of functioning as an assembly. As a consequence, parliaments cannot be allowed to expand indefinitely, or even in strict proportion to population. Hence, the following hypothesis:

> The size of parliaments increases with the population of a country, but at a lower rate.

Table 5.1 shows the population elasticity of parliamentary hypothesis. For all the nations of the world and for 29 democra-

TABLE 5.1

Population and Parliamentary Size, 1970

Category	Population elasticity of parliamentary size	Standard error of elasticity	Percentage of variance explained statistically
29 democracies[a]	.41	.04	76.0%
135 countries	.40	.02	71.7%
50 U.S. state legislatures	.20	.06	20.8%
44 U.S. state legislatures (New England omitted)	.27	.04	50.0%

[a] For the criteria used to choose the 29 democracies, see Robert A. Dahl, *Polyarchy* (New Haven, 1971), Appendix A.

cies, the estimated elasticities indicate that a population difference between countries of 1.0 per cent is associated with a difference in parliamentary size of 0.4 per cent. Thus parliamentary size increases as the number of citizens increases, but it grows more slowly than population. Figure 5.1 shows the relationship for all the countries of the world in 1970.

Although population is not the only explanation of parliamentary size, it is by far the most powerful. Table 5.2 shows a regression equation that explains more than 95 per cent of the variation in parliamentary size for 29 relatively democratic countries. Population size is clearly the most important describing variable; taken alone it describes 76 per cent of the variation in parliamentary size. The smallest country, Iceland, has a parliament with 40 members; the largest democracy, India, has 523 parliamentarians. The regression further indicates that countries with rapidly increasing populations tend to have smaller parliaments than predicted by their absolute size; that countries with multiparty systems tend to have larger parliaments (other things being equal, two-party systems have parliaments averaging about 137 seats; multiparty systems, 195 seats); and that unicameral parliaments are typically somewhat larger than the size for a variety of political units—and the results support the lower house of bicameral parliaments.

Figure 5.2 shows the predicted parliamentary size and the actual size for the 29 countries. Israel, Sweden, and Lebanon all

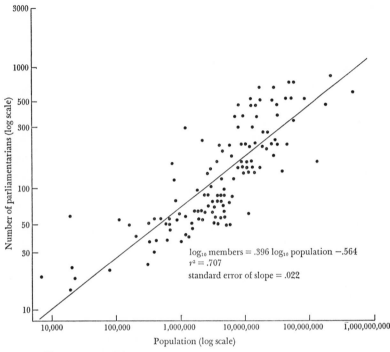

Fig. 5.1. Population and parliamentary size in 135 countries, 1970.

have parliaments that are "too big"; the fitted equation considerably underestimates size of those parliaments. Chile and particularly the Netherlands have considerably smaller parliaments than predicted on the basis of population, population growth rate, the structure of the party system, and the number of houses of parliament. Local political arrangements explain some of the larger residuals. The Netherlands has had a small parliament throughout its history, and the First Chamber has, upon occasion, voted down provisions for an increase in the size of the Second Chamber. Sweden, until late 1970, had a lower house of 233 deputies, which hardly differs from the predicted value. The new, recently instituted unicameral legislature consists of 310 members directly elected in a system of proportional representation. Forty other seats are then filled, in order to bring the distribution of seats received by each party more in line with

TABLE 5.2

Factors Influencing Parliamentary Size in 29 Democracies

Factors	Regression coefficient	Standard error	Relative influence of factors	R_i^2
Population (log)	.440	.022	1.22	.14
Annual population growth rate	−.135	.020	.34	.13
Number of political parties	.051	.013	.16	.26
Bicameral–unicameral	.066	.040	.05	.20

NOTE: $R^2 = .952$. All coefficients are statistically significant at the .001 level, with the exception of the variable bicameral–unicameral. That coefficient is significantly different from zero at the .06 level. R_i^2 is the squared multiple correlation resulting from the regression of the ith describing (independent) variable against all the remaining describing variables. It provides an assessment of multicollinearity, since it indicates how entangled each describing variable is with the remaining describing variables. The relative influence of X_i is $b_i w_i / w_y$, where b_i is the regression coefficient for X_i, w_i is the range of X_i, and w_y is the range of the observed dependent variable. For further discussion see Cuthbert Daniel and Fred S. Wood, *Fitting Equations to Data* (New York, 1971).

the distribution of votes received by each party—thereby reducing the usual inflation of the leading party's share of votes into a larger share of the seats.

Finally, it appears that governmental institutions in general —not just parliaments—tend to grow somewhat more slowly

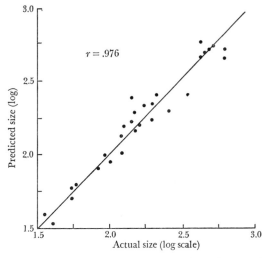

Fig. 5.2. Predicted and actual parliamentary size in 29 democracies, 1970.

than the number of citizens in a political unit. The population elasticity of the number of governmental employees in national and in state governments tends to be slightly less than unity. This perhaps contributes to the distance between citizens and public servants as the size of the political unit grows.

Distance and Distortion

If we reflect on the fact that by our various solutions, communication becomes more asymmetrical; elected leadership becomes less an avocation and more a professional, full-time occupation; leaders become more specialized; the number of constituents per representative increases; communication is more indirect, and subleaders intervene in communications, then it is reasonable to expect that representatives will become less "representative" in several senses of the term. Thus:

> The greater the number of constituents per representative, the greater the differences in social characteristics—occupation, education, income, and the like—between representative and constituents.

Because of the overriding impact of other factors, however, it is doubtful whether these hypothetical consequences of size would show up among democratic countries. In any case, we have no cross-national data. The best study within a country is the Swedish local government study mentioned earlier. Councillors elected to communal councils do in fact diverge more from their constituents in social characteristics as the size of the commune increases. For one thing, differences in income grow markedly (see Table 5.3). Similar differences are found with respect to educational differences between citizens and councillors.

Differences in social and economic characteristics do not, of course, necessarily prevent effective representation of constituents' views. From the perspective of democratic theory, the representation of views is obviously a far more relevant test of representativeness, and thus of citizen effectiveness. Yet size also creates barriers for representation of views. The greater homo-

TABLE 5.3

Median Family Income among Elected Councillors
and Voters, Sweden, 1966

(Swedish crowns; one Sw crown = $.20)

Density of commune	Population of commune			
	Under 8,000	8,000–30,000	Over 30,000	Göteborg (450,000)
Thickly populated:				
Councillors	29,700	34,700	37,900	51,800
Voters	21,300	20,100	21,000	23,700
Difference	8,400	14,600	16,900	28,100
Mixed:				
Councillors	23,500	29,000		
Voters	16,100	18,000		
Difference	7,400	11,000		
Sparsely populated:				
Councillors	22,300			
Voters	18,000			
Difference	3,500			

SOURCE: Lars Strömberg, unpublished data from the councillor-voter study, Local Government Research Group, University of Göteborg.

geneity of the smaller community increases the chance that an elected representative will hold the attitudes of his constituents—even without further communication after he has been elected. Any increase in the number of constituents makes it more difficult to achieve an accurate match between the views of voters and politicians. Finally, the possibility of divergence in attitudes and views is enhanced by increased social differences, combined with more indirect chains of communication and dependence on subleaders for conveying views about citizens' preferences. Thus it is a persuasive hypothesis that:

The greater the number of constituents a representative has, the greater is likely to be the divergence in policies between representative and constituents.

In the Swedish study, the only direct test available to us, it was found that elected councillors in the larger communes diverged more from constituents in attitudes toward local taxes than coun-

TABLE 5.4

Positive Attitude Toward Local Taxes among Socialist and Non-Socialist Councillors and Voters

(Mean percentage per commune within respective groups of those prepared to raise local taxes)

| | Population of commune | | | | | |
| | Under 8,000 | | 8,000–30,000 | | Over 30,000 | |
Density of commune	Non-Soc.	Soc.	Non-Soc.	Soc.	Non-Soc.	Soc.
Thickly populated:						
Councillors	16%	24%	19%	62%	21%	64%
Voters	15%	19%	14%	20%	16%	16%
Mixed:						
Councillors	24%	53%	22%	52%		
Voters	25%	23%	17%	29%		
Sparsely populated:						
Councillors	11%	32%				
Voters	20%	30%				

SOURCE: See Table 5.3.

cillors in the small, compact communes. The views of Socialist councillors were particularly discrepant in the large communes (see Table 5.4). A comparison between voters and councillors as to what local services should have the highest priority also revealed that in the small, densely populated communes, agreement on priorities was greatest; agreement on priorities decreased with increasing size and decreasing densities. However, to place these differences in perspective, it should be added that even in the larger communes the degree of agreement was remarkably great. Probably party competition in the larger communes helped to keep the councillors in line with constituent opinion; we shall return to this conjecture in the next chapter, for it is crucial to a full explanation of the consequences of size for citizen effectiveness.

Summary

Large differences in the number of citizens in a representative democracy have consequences for participation and communication. A highly simplified presentation of these consequences would look something like this:

In representative democracies:

The smaller the scale of the society, the more likely it is that:	The larger the scale of the society, the more likely it is that:
1. An ordinary citizen can deal directly with a top leader if he chooses to do so.	1. An ordinary citizen cannot deal directly with a top leader but must go through various channels of communication.
2. Leaders gain their information about citizens' wants by direct observation and communication.	2. Leaders depend on subordinates or groups who summarize information about citizens' wants.
3. Leaders directly oversee the actions of subleaders.	3. Subleaders acquire autonomy, de facto or de jure.
4. Communication between citizens and leaders is reciprocal.	4. Communication is asymmetric: top leaders communicate directly by electronic means with more and more citizens, whereas an increasing proportion of citizens cannot communicate directly with top leaders.
5. Top leaders communicate directly with one another.	5. Top leaders communicate with one another through intermediaries, if at all.
6. Top leaders are less functionally specialized: they accumulate roles.	6. Top leaders are more functionally specialized: they occupy particular roles.
7. Top leaders have occupations or roles outside of politics that provide them with opportunities to engage in politics, but less than full-time.	7. Top leaders are professional politicians whose main occupation is politics, and nearly all of whose roles are political.

Thus larger-scale politics necessarily limits democracy in one respect: the larger the scale of politics, the less able is the average citizen to deal directly with his top political leaders. Moreover, larger-scale politics generates an increasing asymmetry in relations between citizens and top leaders: not only are citizens likely to have less knowledge about politics than their leaders, but communications are necessarily more and more asymmetrical. It might well be true, then, that:

> In order to minimize differences in power, knowledge, and directness of two-way communication between citizens and national leaders, a necessary but not sufficient condition is that the political system be small.

> In order to generate marked differences in power, knowledge, and directness of two-way communication between citizens and national leaders, a sufficient but not necessary condition is that the political system be large.

Unfortunately, these theoretical conjectures are extraordinarily difficult to test, not only because of the data measurement problems, but also because of the difficulty of distinguishing in practice between necessary and sufficient conditions. To repeat the theoretical propositions so as to avoid misinterpretation, we conjecture that:

> Only in smaller-scale politics can differences in power, knowledge, and directness of communication between citizens and top leaders be reduced to a minimum.

> In larger-scale politics the irreducible differences in power, knowledge, and directness of communication are necessarily greater than in smaller-scale politics.

> But factors other than size, such as political culture, may prevent smaller systems from reducing differences between citizens and leaders to the theoretical minimum for smaller systems.

SIX

Competition, Conflict, and Responsiveness

Until comparatively recent times, dissent, diversity, and conflict were usually regarded as unequivocal dangers to republics. As we saw in the first chapter, right through the American Constitutional Convention, republics were thought to be peculiarly subject to the terrible and often fatal disease of faction. A small republic might escape the disease, as Montesquieu argued, because homogeneity would make for a strong and healthy body politic. But a large republic would be destroyed by "an internal vice": conflict. In Chapter 1 we saw Madison brilliantly turn that argument on its head, making smallness into a vice, largeness into a virtue. In doing so, however, he bypassed the important question we have explored in the last two chapters, the consequences of size for citizen effectiveness. To be sure, a large republic might be able to handle factionalism; but would not its citizens be less effective, its officials more remote and less responsive?

The answer, as we began to hint in Chapter 4, is that increasing size may have contradictory consequences for citizen effectiveness. We have presented theoretical and empirical foundations for the perspective that in the tradition of Rousseau emphasizes the advantages of smallness for citizen effectiveness. We now turn to an opposing perspective, Madisonian, if you like, which, having accepted the need for larger units of government and therefore the necessity of representative rather than direct democracy, emphasizes the aspects of large size that facilitate citizen effectiveness. Among these is greater density of population and, as a consequence, larger chances for dissent and opposition to find expression and representation.

If increasing numbers seem to dilute the effectiveness of the average citizen, there is one way in which increasing numbers work to enhance his effectiveness: by increasing the chances of finding an ally.

The famous experiments on conformity by the psychologist S. E. Asch show that in small groups the likelihood that a given individual will maintain a dissenting view increases considerably if at least one other person joins him in dissent. In small groups, then, the ability to find an ally is important if dissent is to be expressed. For larger aggregates, it seems a truism that the ability to find an ally or allies—to build a coalition—is vitally important for success in obtaining political rewards. How is size related to the ability to build a coalition?

Let us assume, in line with the Asch experiments, that a divergent minority in a political system must be larger than a certain minimum size if it is to communicate, organize, and express its dissent. Conceivably, this minimum size—the threshold for dissent—may be a proportion, a minimum number or, more likely, some combination of the two. Suppose, for example, that if dissenters are less than 10 per cent and less than 10,000 in number, they will tend to remain silent, but whenever they exceed 10,000, no matter what proportion they are of the total population, they will tend to coalesce and express their dissent. These possibilities suggest three lines of theoretical argument.

1. If the threshold to dissent is a minimum number and if the proportion of dissenters tends to remain the same, then obviously the larger a polity the more likely the number of dissenters will exceed the threshold. This line of argument applies both among countries and to communities within countries.

2. If the threshold is a minimum *proportion*, then it is plausible to argue on purely statistical grounds that *within* a country, the chances of finding an ally should increase with the size of a community. Let us assume that the threshold of dissent is a proportion—20 per cent, say, must be dissenters if they are to become mobilized politically. Now, large samples repeatedly give more stable estimates of the population mean than do small samples. If 30 per cent of the people in a country are dissenters, and if we

repeatedly draw samples of size 100, in very few of the samples will the proportion of dissenters deviate by more than a few percentage points from the mean of 30 per cent for the whole country. In fact in groups of 100 drawn randomly from this population, less than 2 per cent of the groups are likely to be below the threshold for dissent. The smaller the sample, however, the greater the variability: among groups of 10, for example, more than a third will be below the threshold. Thus, insofar as communities are random samples of the whole population of a country, the smaller the community the greater the chance that its divergent minority will be below the threshold for dissent.

3. A final line of argument flows out of the conjecture we explored in Chapter 3, that the number and diversity of organizations in a polity increases with size. In a town of 2,000, there is one plumber and no organized plumber's interest; in a city of two million, there is not only a plumber's union but in addition many other organized interests (not found in smaller polities) that can join with the plumber's union in pursuit of mutual benefits.

These arguments lend support to two hypotheses:

The greater the number of members in a democratic political system, the greater the chance that a dissenter will find enough allies to pass the threshold for dissent.

As the number of members in a democratic political system increases, the likelihood of persistent and overt opposition to majority views also increases.

From the Politics of Homogeneity to the Politics of Diversity

With increasing size, then, persistent and overt differences in political outlooks, interests, and demands are likely to appear. The small system, being more homogeneous, is, as Rousseau and Montesquieu assumed, likely to be more consensual; the larger system, being more heterogeneous, is, as they predicted, likely to be more conflictual. Thus the style of political life changes; and if the larger polity is not to founder in a sea of turbulence, it must develop new, more elaborate, more formal, more highly organized institutions for dealing with conflicts. A paradigm (which of course drastically simplifies reality) might look something like this:

	In smaller systems:	In larger systems:
1. The members are more	homogeneous	diverse
2. Incentives to conform to a uniform code of behavior are	stronger	weaker
3. In relation to the numbers holding the majority view in a conflict, the number who openly dissent are	fewer	greater
4. The likelihood that conflicts among groups involve personal conflicts among the individuals in each group is	higher	lower
5. Conversely, conflicts among organizations are	less frequent	more frequent
6. Processes for dealing with organized group conflicts are	less institutionalized	more institutionalized
7. Group conflicts are	infrequent but explosive	frequent but less explosive
8. Group conflicts are	more likely to polarize the whole community	less likely to polarize the whole community

The first proposition in the paradigm is, of course, only a reassertion of our argument in Chapter 3. The second is widely held to be true. If a system is both small and homogeneous, variations in behavior are fewer, a higher percentage of the population adheres to a single code, the norms of the code are easily communicated by word and example, violations are visible, sanctions are easy to apply by means of both gross and subtle forms of social interaction, and avoidance of sanctions is difficult. By contrast, growing division of labor breaks down this kind of primal soli-

darity; a single code of behavior is inapplicable; with growing
numbers and territory, anonymity and avoidance of sanctions are
easier; and heterogeneous systems develop diverse and often conflicting codes of behavior.[1] Thus, as we argued a moment ago, it
becomes easier for a dissenter to find allies; reinforced by increasing diversity, oppositions grow in relative size.

In the smaller system, any conflict among organized groups is
likely to entail personal conflicts among the individuals in the
groups. Individuals cannot take refuge in anonymity. Each knows
the other's group affiliations. Hence a group conflict, particularly
if it endures for long, is likely to reinforce—and be reinforced by
—personal antagonisms. In the larger system, on the other hand,
the individuals in the antagonistic groups are much less likely to
confront one another, and, indeed, may never meet.

If individuals in the smaller system foresee that whenever
group conflict emerges they will have to pay dearly for it in their
personal relationships, conflict is likely to be less frequent than
in the larger system. Organized group conflict entails extra costs
in the form of individual antagonisms among people who must
frequently confront one another. Moreover, homogeneity re-
duces the number of available nodes around which group life
can form. The plumber is not an organized interest. The small,
homogeneous system is simply less "groupy"; group loyalties are
correspondingly weaker, whereas overall solidarity is greater.
Hence if group conflict is to be pressed, the stakes, both personal
and collective, need to be relatively higher in the small system
than in the large one. And in the small system, the further group
conflict is pressed, the higher the stakes become.

Because group conflicts are infrequent and dangerous in small
systems, they are more likely to be ad hoc than institutionalized.
Organizations spring up in response to a conflict, and die out
when it ends. In the larger system, where group conflicts are frequent and far less costly to the individual members, the advan-

[1] This is a restatement of some of Durkheim's views in *The Division of Labor
in Society* (New York, 1960). See, however, the modification proposed by Allardt,
"A Theory on Solidarity and Legitimacy Conflicts," in E. Allardt and Y. Littunen,
eds., *Cleavages, Ideologies and Parity Systems* (Helsinki, 1964), pp. 78–96.

tages of permanent, organized institutions for dealing with conflict are more obvious; hence group conflicts are likely to take on institutionalized forms.

Consequently, when group conflicts do occur in the smaller system, they are likely to be explosive. New organizations arise. New leaders, inexperienced in managing conflict, confront one another. Personal antagonisms run high. Ancient but long-suppressed personal resentments erupt. The initial issues in the controversy rapidly expand and, as the dispute waxes, may even be totally lost. Disagreement turns into a quarrel — and a family quarrel at that.

If the cost of conflict is high in the small system, the price of neutrality is higher. The neutral is not only perfectly visible but, in the emotional, inflamed atmosphere of the conflict, likely to be perceived as an enemy by both sides. Threatened by isolation, he may find it better to break some ties than to rupture all his friendships. As more issues are involved, more and more individuals and groups find a reason for joining the fray. Hence the smaller system—particularly if it is a territorial community such as a village or a town—is likely to become more fully polarized into two warring camps than the larger system, where anonymity, indifference, impersonality, lack of direct ties, even lack of knowledge, all make it possible for a large part of the population to sit it out.

Problems

This, then, is the paradigm and the reasoning that makes it persuasive. Four problems, however, remain. First, it is quite likely that the characteristics we think describe conflict in smaller systems are associated in a significant way only with *very small* systems—with towns, say, having a population of under 10,000. Whatever this threshold may be, it is, most likely, lower than the population of even a very small country like Iceland. If this is so, then in all democratic countries conflict would tend to have the characteristics ascribed to "larger systems"; hence the paradigm would tell us nothing about cross-national differences in patterns of conflict. And indeed, the available qualitative and impressionistic evidence indicates that among the smaller European democracies, conflict does *not* have the characteristics ascribed in our paridigm to "smaller systems"; on the contrary, these countries seem to fit mainly the description of conflict in "larger" systems. So far as the paradigm is concerned, even most subunits—towns, cities, states, provinces—may be "larger" systems.

Second, at the level of nation-states we confront, as always, the unique historical legacy of each nation, which may account far better than size differences can for the observed cross-national variations in conflict management. For example, variations in the patterns of handling political conflict in Sweden, the Netherlands, Britain, and the United States seem more closely related to historical development than to differences in size. Thus we must look for comparative evidence within rather than among representative democracies.

Third, even within a country it is difficult to sort out the unique effects of size (population) on diversity, dissent, and party competition, because more populous units tend to be not merely larger but more urbanized and "modern." The extent of diversity in a political unit is clearly a function of at least two different sets of factors: unique historical influences, which as we have just said are particularly noticeable at the level of nation-states, and social-organizational factors, particularly size, and especially the size of the population; the extent of specialization of labor and other resources, which in turn is a function of industrialization and other aspects of economic development; and density of population particularly as measured by degree of urbanization.

The social-organizational factors are highly intercorrelated. In fact, they generally reflect a developmental pattern in which comprehensive systemic changes are occurring: the shift from small, preindustrial, agrarian communities to large, urban centers characterized by industry, commerce, and specialized services, and the proliferation of urban and "modern" institutions of all kinds, from mass education to mass communications. Among the modern institutions characteristic of this kind of society are competitive political parties. It follows that even in a relatively small unit, urbanization, industrialization, and increasing socioeconomic complexity are likely to lead to more highly organized party competition, and to styles and forms of politics in general that are characteristic of larger units. In short, the more modern the society of the small unit, the more modern its political organizations, and particularly its parties. But since larger units are likely to be more modern, they compound and confound the effects of size. In theory the effects can be sorted out; in practice, with the data available, they sometimes cannot.

Fourth, then, we must face the problem of how the paradigm can be interpreted in order to test it, and how valid it would appear after adequate testing. Taken together, several propositions in the paradigm suggest some hypotheses that might be fruitfully examined. The fifth and sixth propositions in the paradigm are certainly crucial. As overt conflict becomes an everyday feature of political life, institutionalized processes are necessary to prevent controversy from escalating into conflict so violent and explosive as to destroy the democratic regime itself. It is the organization and institutionalization of conflict resolution in the larger system that helps to produce the consequences expressed in the seventh and eighth propositions. The serpent of conflict is regularly drained of its venom.

For reasons we have already indicated, the country is probably too large a unit for testing the paradigm. To detect the effects of size on conflict, we must therefore look within countries. We hypothesize that:

1. Within a country governed by a system of representative democracy, the larger the political unit the greater the extent to which public conflict is expressed and resolved through formal and impersonal organizations rather than through informal, face-to-face negotiations by the antagonists themselves.

The most visible and in many ways the most important organization involved in conflict resolution in representative democracies is of course the political party. Considering our fifth and sixth propositions in the light of the third, we would expect that in larger systems political parties would not only be more deeply involved in the everyday management of conflict than in smaller systems; they would also be more evenly balanced in their struggles. For if the third proposition is correct, the dissenters from the majority view would form a larger proportion of the total, and the minority party or parties would be less overshadowed by the majority party or coalition than would be the case in smaller systems. Indeed, our paradigm suggests that in the politics of homogeneity parties scarcely exist. And as they begin to appear in the small community, homogeneity initially tends to insure the dominance of a single party. The small community, then, is likely to be a one-party system.

As heterogeneity increases—and size, we have argued, contributes to and is associated with greater heterogeneity—one-party dominance declines and other parties gain a following among those who dissent from the majority perspective. As partisan conflict gains legitimacy, and as heterogeneity increases further, the parties become more nearly equal competitors. Hence we conjecture that:

2. Within a given democracy, the larger the political unit, the greater the relative size of the minority party or parties.

Organizations

Two studies provide evidence bearing on the first of the two hypotheses we have just advanced. Eyestone and Eulau[2] sent questionnaires to all the councilmen in 88 cities in the San Francisco Bay Region. They received replies from 60 per cent of these officials. Among other things, the councilmen were asked to rate as "high," "moderate," "low," or "not applicable" the degree of participation in city politics by different organizations. The organizations were classified in nine categories, ranging "from chambers of commerce and trade unions to library associations and neighborhood clubs." As Table 6.1 shows, the councilmen from the larger cities reported considerably more organized activity than the councilmen from the smaller cities and towns.

[2] Robert Eyestone and Heinz Eulau, "City Councils and Policy Outcomes: Developmental Profiles," in James Q. Wilson, ed., *City Politics and Public Policy* (New York, 1968), pp. 37–65.

TABLE 6.1

City Size and Organizational Participation in Politics,
San Francisco Bay Region

	City size	
Number of categories rated high	Over 25,000 ($N = 104$)	Under 25,000 ($N = 145$)
0–2	8%	51%
3–5	58	42
6–9	34	7
TOTAL	100%	100%

NOTE: N = number of councilmen who returned the questionnaire in each size category.

The Swedish local-government study furnishes much more detailed support for our hypothesis. In the smaller communes in general, the level of formal, organizational activity is low, whereas the level of personal contacts is high. In the larger communes, by contrast, pressure groups are more active, organizations play a greater part, and the parties in a particular commune are more active, more "political," more often the locus of political discussion and the source of political proposals and demands (see Table 6.2).

What comes through rather sharply in Table 6.2 is a persistent tendency for organizational and partisan activity to increase in importance with the size of the commune. Density works in the same direction; thus while the smaller communes are less organized and less partisan than the larger, among the smaller communes the least densely populated ones, presumably rural areas, tend to be even less organized and partisan than the more densely populated small towns.

Party Competition: The Netherlands

As with nearly every other hypothesis about the consequences of size for political institutions and activities, our second hypothesis is complicated by the effects of other causal factors. If heterogeneity, dissent, and partisanship increase with size, this is partly because increasing size is associated with other factors that facilitate political diversity and its expression. Among these are urbanization and the high densities of urban life, and the increas-

TABLE 6.2
*Population Size, Population Density, Organizational Participation in
Politics, and Partisan Activity in Swedish Communes, 1966*

Criterion of activity (yearly basis)	Is lowest where		Is highest where	
	Density is	Population is	Density is	Population is
Number of membership meetings of organizations at which local political questions are discussed	low	low	high or mixed	high or medium
Average rate of attendance among organizations	low	low	high	high
Number of times requests presented to the communal council by organizations	low	low	high	high
Number of ad hoc groups presenting requests to the council	high	low	mixed or high	medium or high
Number of membership meetings in party organizations	mixed or low	low	high	high
Number of general meetings of local party branches	mixed	low	high	high
Proportion of local party organization meetings that discuss questions to to be taken up by the local council	low	low	high	high
Proportion of local party organizations instructing their council representatives on positions	mixed	low	high	high
Per cent of split-ticket voting, 1966 local election	high	high	mixed or high	medium or low
Perception by council members of distance between parties	low	low	high	high

SOURCE: See Table 5.3, p. 85.

ing degree of specialization and differentiation of labor and other resources that tend to distinguish town from country, city from town, metropolis from city. In addition, the electoral system has a significant effect on the opportunities for minorities to express themselves through parties. Consequently, we need to make our second hypothesis more specific:

2*a*. Among political units within a democratic country, diversity and competition among political parties increase with the size of the unit, the degree of urbanization, and the degree of specialization and differentiation of labor and other resources.

2*b*. Among political units within a democratic country where a system of proportional representation obtains, the number of parties (or party lists) presented to the voters at election increases with unit size, degree of urbanization, degree of specialization, and differentiation of labor and other resources.

2*c*. Among political units within a democratic country where a system of proportional representation obtains, the percentage of the vote cast for the leading party decreases with unit size, degree of urbanization, and degree of societal differentiation.

The relationships asserted in these three subordinate hypotheses are presented in Figure 6.1.

Hypothesis 2*a* is supported by an analysis of data from the 1962 municipal elections in the Netherlands (Table 6.3), in which the municipalities are classified according to several characteristics—chiefly population, population density, and employment in agriculture and industry. As the table shows, the number of party lists offered to the voters in the 1962 municipal elections increased quite steadily from the smallest agricultural communities to the largest cities. The only significant anomaly is presented by the urbanized rural municipalities that contain small cities; the anomaly is largely an artifact of the typology, however, for in size and

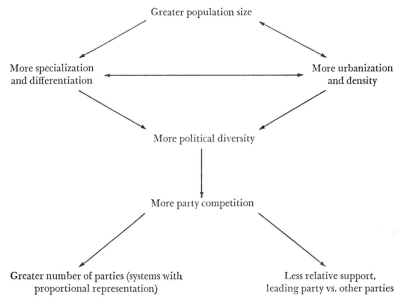

Fig. 6.1. Hypothetical relation between population size and party competition. (The arrows represent the hypothetical causal relation and may be read as "leads to" or "produces.")

industrialization these communities are much like small or medium-sized cities.

This tendency of the smaller or less economically developed units to present fewer lists restricts not only the absolute number of parties their voters may choose among, but also in some cases the availability of at least one party list from each of the four main "spiritual families" of the Netherlands—Catholic, Protestant, liberal, and socialist. A large city probably will offer its voters party lists from all four "families," whereas a smaller or more rural community may lack a list from one or more of them (Table 6.3).

The difference between the small rural community and the large city, then, might be put this way: Every party, no matter what spiritual family it belongs to, is much more likely to compete in the larger city than in the small town or the countryside; every party that competes in the village, town, or countryside is very likely to compete also in the city, and it almost certainly

TABLE 6.3

Size, Urbanization, and Political Diversity in the Netherlands,
Municipal Elections of 1962

(Total $N = 962$)

Urbanization and size	Average number of party lists	Representation of spiritual families	
		Per cent with lists from all 4	Per cent lacking one or more
Rural municipalities, by % males in agriculture:			
Over 50% $(N = 96)$	3.75	12% ⎫	
40–50% $(N = 159)$	4.24	14 ⎪	
30–40% $(N = 187)$	4.63	16 ⎬ 61%	
20–30% $(N = 145)$	4.79	17 ⎭	
Urbanized rural municipalities, with over 80% in nonagricultural occupations:			
Over 50% males in manufacturing, and largest population cluster:			
Under 5,000 $(N = 120)$	5.17	12% ⎫ 21%	
10,000–30,000 $(N = 85)$	6.60	38 ⎭	
Suburbs: over 30% commuters $(N = 54)$	5.48	80	6
Urban municipalities (densely populated, contiguous built-up areas):			
Country towns: 2,000–10,000 $(N = 38)$	5.32	54% ⎫ 3	
Small towns: 10,000–30,000 $(N = 38)$	6.03	71 ⎭	
Cities: 30,000–50,000 $(N = 11)$	6.64	55 ⎫	
50,000–100,000 $(N = 17)$	7.29	88 ⎬ 8%	
Over 100,000 $(N = 12)$	7.92	100 ⎭ 1	

SOURCE: Central Bureau voor de Statistiek, *Typologie van de Nederlandse gemeenten naar ur-banisatie-graad, 31 mei 1960* (Typologies of the Netherlands Municipalities According to Degree of Urbanization, May 31, 1960) (Zeist, 1964), pp. 18ff. The categories of urbanization are those used in the source.

competes in big cities; but parties that compete in big cities frequently do not compete in countryside, village, or town.[3]

It is not at all surprising that the socialist parties often fail to submit lists in rural areas, or that much the same thing holds for the members of the liberal spiritual family, rooted as it is in the urban educated classes. But it is somewhat surprising that even the religious parties are more likely to compete in the cities than in the rural communities. For example, no Protestant list was presented in a third of the rural communities in 1962, whereas every large city offered at least one Protestant list. Moreover, competition among two or more Protestant parties was more frequent in the urban areas than elsewhere.

Switzerland

Data from the Swiss cantons also lend support to our hypothesis about size and diversity. The larger a canton in area and population, the denser its population, and the more highly developed it is economically, the greater the number of parties represented in its delegation to the National Council of the Federal Assembly. The correlation between population and number of parties represented is extraordinarily high (0.89), because fewer parties compete in elections in the smaller cantons and fewer of those represented who do compete succeed in getting delegates elected. The main relationships and the correlation coefficients involved here are shown in Figure 6.2a.

The hypothesis is again supported when we consider the number of parties represented in each of the 25 cantonal legislative bodies (Grands Conseils). Although area is relatively unimpor-

[3] The size of a municipal council in the Netherlands is determined by the population of its constituency, from seven members in municipalities with fewer than 3,000 people to 45 members in municipalities with more than 200,000 people. It is difficult to estimate the effect of council size on the incentives to submit a list. Since the larger the council the smaller the percentage of the vote needed to win a seat, it could be argued that the parties have stronger incentives to offer a list in the larger communities. On the other hand, since the larger the city the larger the absolute number of votes needed (e.g. 1,000 votes per seat in a city of 10,000; 2,700 votes in a city of 100,000; almost 4,500 votes in a city of 200,000), it could be argued that the incentive would be greater in the smaller cities. We do not know how to weigh the importance of these tactical considerations, but they should be kept in mind.

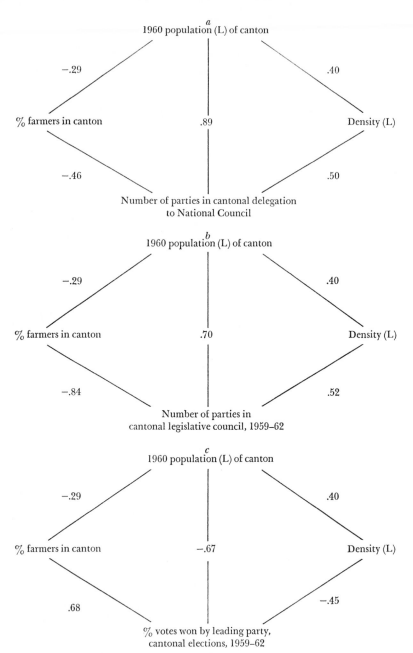

Fig. 6.2. Population, population density, percentage of agricultural employment, and political diversity in 25 Swiss cantons, 1959–62.

tant, the number of parties in the cantonal legislature depends heavily on the population of the canton, its density, and the percentage of its population employed in nonagricultural occupations (Figure 6.2b).

So far we have paid attention only to the number of parties involved in the political process. What is to be said about partisan predominance or competitiveness as indicated by the percentage of the vote cast for the leading party? We have no data on the Netherlands, but party competition in Switzerland is consistent with our hypothesis 2c. For example, the percentage of the votes cast for the leading party in elections to each of the cantonal legislatures is likely to be higher in the smaller, less densely populated, more agricultural cantons (Fig. 6.2c). In short, the smaller the canton, the more homogeneous its voters are likely to be. Indeed, the parties seem to be less competitive in every respect in the smaller, more agrarian cantons than in the larger, more urbanized cantons.[4] Girod has classified the 25 cantons in several ways. In one classification by party competitiveness, he divides them into cantons with (1) solitary or predominant party and (2) three parties or a pronounced multiparty system. He has also classified them into four categories according to the extent to which the incumbents on the executive council of the canton are challenged by opponents in their reelection efforts. The grounds of this classification are not altogether clear; we have combined two categories consisting of cantons in which the government is regularly reelected without opposition. Girod's first classification leads to correlations almost exactly the same as correlations with the percentage of votes for the leading party, but naturally in the opposite direction. Girod's second classification results in lower coefficients, but all in the appropriate direction.

	Per cent of vote for leading party	Party dominance	Contested elections
Population (log)	−.67	.61	.45
Per cent farmers	.68	−.69	−.26
Population density (log)	−.45	.41	.25
Area (log)	−.24	.19	.18

[4] Roger Girod, "Geography of the Swiss Party System," in Allardt and Littunen, pp. 132–61.

The United States: The 50 States

The specific hypotheses we have been testing were formulated to apply to countries with systems of proportional representation. But if our general theoretical notions about size and political diversity are valid, then they should also apply to democratic countries with two-party systems, or indeed to any democratic system and even to political units within a democratic country. But since our hypotheses were restricted to countries with proportional representation, we need to formulate some equivalent hypotheses appropriate to countries with single-member districts and two parties: fortunately our basic hypothesis (2*a*) can be rephrased to serve the purpose with little change:

> 2*a′*. Among political units within a democratic country having plurality elections where practically all votes are cast for one of two parties (as in the United States), the extent to which the two parties compete in the various units increases with the size of the unit, the degree of urbanization, and the degree of specialization and differentiation of labor and other resources.

The United States offers a variety of units for testing the hypothesis—states, counties, and cities, among others. We shall offer evidence drawn from the states.

However, although the two-party system is something of a reality in most of the North, as everyone knows in the South the Republican party has until recently been so weak and ill-organized that it was more a political wraith than a party to be reckoned with. The one-party South has been a massive reality in American politics. This reality now appears to be changing; but on any of the usual measures of party competition the South still shows up as a markedly different region from the rest of the country. In comparing North and South we witness, as with different countries, the effects of a unique historical legacy that may well overwhelm the weaker factors we are exploring. Consequently, we shall separate the South from the rest of the country.

The 35 states outside the South are large and heterogeneous entities. In 1960 the average non-Southern state had a population

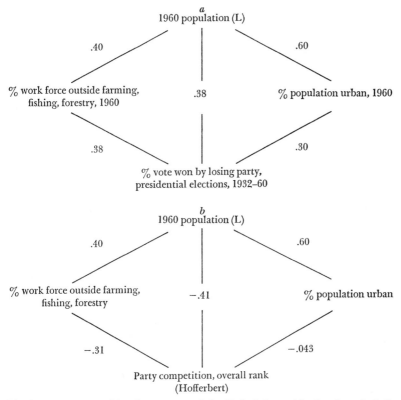

Fig. 6.3. Party competition in 35 states of the United States (the South excluded), 1932–60. In part *b*, since the most competitive party ranks 1 and the least competitive 50, negative coefficients mean that the variable is associated with a higher degree of party competition.

of nearly 3.7 million and an area of 63,000 square miles: in area, then, about five times as large as Belgium or the Netherlands, twice the size of Austria, half as large as Norway, and a third as large as Sweden.

Even among these 35 states, however, the main relationships hold up. Although the relationships are not strong, population, urbanization, and employment outside farming, fishing, and forestry are all associated with a higher degree of party competition. In Figure 6.3*a* we have used as a measure of party competition the percentage of the vote gained by the losing party in presidential elections from 1932 to 1960. The coefficients indicate that

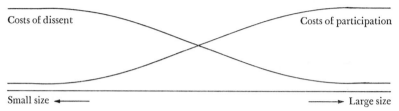

Fig. 6.4. Size and the costs of dissent and participation.

presidential elections are less one-sided in the larger, more urbanized, less agricultural states. Other measures of party competition show similar relationships. In Figure 6.3*b* we show the relationships with Hofferbert's overall ranking of party competition in the states, which is based upon nine different measures.[5]

Citizen Effectiveness: Conclusion

In Chapter 2 we cautioned that there is a trade-off between our two major criteria, the effectiveness of the citizen and the capacity of the system. As we reflect on the argument of the last three chapters, it is evident that the criteria of citizen effectiveness itself calls for an estimate of trade-offs between two different aspects of effectiveness: the costs of participation and communication, and the costs of dissent. As the number of citizens in a "democratic" polity increases beyond the size of a committee or a village, the costs of participation and communication with leaders increase. But the costs of dissent decline; or to put it differently, there is a greater chance of finding an ally in dissent and an opportunity to participate in an organization with policies deviating from majority views. The general thrust of our conclusion is shown in Figure 6.4.

Now it might be thought that the optimum size for a democratic polity would be at the intersection of the two curves. But there are two objections to this facile proposal. In the first place,

[5] Richard Hofferbert, "Classification of American State Party Systems," *Journal of Politics* 26 (1964), 550–67. Hofferbert's overall ranking is based on three types of elections, 1932–62: presidential, senatorial, gubernatorial; and, for each type of election, three measures: the percentage of elections won by the leading party, the average per cent of the vote won by the losing party, and the cyclical turnover. All the measures are intercorrelated.

as we have suggested more than once and will argue again in the next chapter, the criterion of system capacity makes small systems too costly for many purposes and thus leads to the need for many systems. To anticipate a conclusion of the next chapter, the criterion of system capacity implies that in the present world there is no single optimum size for democratic polities. In the second place, it must be pointed out that the shape of the curves in Figure 6.4 is highly arbitrary. We have no unit with which to measure the costs, and we do not know where the intersection would be even if we did have such a unit. Figure 6.4 is a picture, not more.

Citizen effectiveness evidently depends on different techniques in the politics of homogeneity of the small system and in the politics of diversity of the large system. In the small democratic system, the chances for citizens to be effective are enhanced by the lower costs of direct communication with representatives and other officials, and by greater homogeneity, which means that even without communication representatives are more likely to hold views like those of their constituents. The large democratic system loses these advantages, as we have seen; it depends more heavily on indirect chains of communication and on overt competition among organized political forces, particularly among parties.

If very small democratic units could satisfy the criterion of system capacity, the politics of homogeneity might, for many people, be more attractive than the politics of diversity. Yet the balance of advantage is very far from clear.

In any case, that option is closed. For to be truly effective, citizens must have political systems with the capacity to deal with matters that citizens regard as important. This will often call for very large systems. Does this mean, then, that small democratic units are, today, inherently unsatisfactory? We now turn to that problem.

SEVEN

Size and System Capacity

To what extent does the size of a democratic system—particularly its population—affect its capacity for dealing with its problems? Is size related to the ability of a democratic system to manipulate and to adapt to its environment? Can large democracies achieve the goals and aspirations of their people more fully than small democracies—or is it the other way around?

By Way of Warning

In the best of circumstances these would be exceptionally difficult questions to answer. And the difficulty is compounded by the biases with which most of us are likely to undertake the search. Just as what one sees in an inkblot may reveal more about one's preconceptions than about the ambiguous inkblot itself, so here our questions are likely to stimulate preconceptions that are then imposed on a highly ambiguous reality.

During the flourishing centuries of the Greek city-states, most literate Greeks seem to have been so strongly biased in favor of the city-state, so little persuaded of any possible virtues in the large state, that they were blinded to the fact that their city-state was a transitory historic form, destined to be superseded. In the last century or so, the tide has run the other way. Today, those who advocate a breakup of the nation-state into city-states are a rare breed who are more likely to be considered eccentric than taken seriously.[1]

[1] Leopold Kohr opens his book *The Breakdown of Nations* (New York, 1957) with this arresting comment: "As the physicists of our time have tried to elaborate

History and nature do not tell us much—except caution. The Greek city-state did, after all, survive as a political form for nearly a thousand years, if we include both its shadowy origins and its senescence. Athens endured longer as a democratic city-state than the United States has yet existed. The Venetian Republic lasted about a thousand years—not a bad record for endurance. If history has seen numerous small states absorbed into large ones, it has also seen the reverse process. The twentieth century has witnessed a good deal of disintegration, particularly of empires, and there are more independent political units claiming sovereignty today than there were at the beginning of this century.

Nature's early experiment with giant forms of life seems to have been disastrous. Yet among mammals a great variety of forms and sizes seems to flourish, ranging in size from the mouse to the whale. A small-democracy man may put his bets on the mouse outlasting the elephant and the whale; doubtless he will find takers among Chinese, Russians, and Americans. But even if we knew that outcome now, it would be hard to know what to make of it.

Let us then turn to our question: How, if at all, is the capacity of a democratic system related to its size, particularly the size of its population? Specifically, how is size related to the capacity of a democratic unit for managing its internal conflicts, for economic and cultural achievement, and for maintaining independence and autonomy against the threat of military aggression and political domination?

We deal briefly with the questions of conflict management and economic and cultural achievement in this chapter. In the next and final chapter we shall consider at greater length the crucial question of independence and autonomy, returning thus to an

---

an integrated single theory, capable of explaining not only some but all phenomena of the *physical* universe, so I have tried on a different plane to develop a single theory through which not only some but all phenomena of the *social* universe can be reduced to a common denominator. The result is a new and unified political philosophy centering in the *theory of size.* It suggests that there seems only one cause behind all forms of social misery: *bigness.* Oversimplified as this may seem, we shall find the idea more easily acceptable if we consider that bigness, or oversize, is really much more than just a social problem. It appears to be the one and only problem permeating all creation. Wherever something is wrong, something is too big."

opening theme that has been heard frequently in these pages. Because the questions we ask are primarily significant—and in any case more manageable—at the level of a country, most of our discussion will be about countries rather than subordinate units within countries.

Internal Conflict

Let us begin by considering the possibility that the fatal *vice intérieur* of a democracy is, as Montesquieu and Madison both argued (but from opposing points of view), the danger of "faction." Is there a reason to believe that the severity of political conflict within a country may be related to its size? For example, if small countries are more homogeneous, might they not be less prone to dangerously bitter conflicts than large heterogeneous countries?

In general, as we saw earlier, cultural diversity is not related to the size of a country's population, though a country of large territory and low population density is more likely to have a high degree of cultural diversity than a country of small area and high densities. For example, the eleven smaller European democracies[2] include not only some of the most homogeneous countries in the world, but also several countries with a very high degree of what Val Lorwin calls segmented pluralism. The homogeneity of a small country is often the product of an historical process of fission that separates a small and relatively less diverse nation from a larger, more heterogeneous polity. Thus among the smaller European democracies, the Netherlands gained independence from Spain and Austria, Belgium from the Netherlands, Norway from Sweden, Finland from Russia, Iceland from Denmark, Ireland from Britain. The further separation of Northern Ireland led to civil war, but also to almost total religious homogeneity in Ireland. Austria is a linguistically homogeneous remnant of a large multi-national empire. Moreover, the seeming vulnerability of small states to aggression from large states, a matter we shall return to in the next chapter, provides strong incentives for internal

[2] Austria, Belgium, Denmark, Finland, Iceland, Ireland, Luxembourg, the Netherlands, Norway, Sweden, Switzerland.

cohesion. Indeed Lijphart argues that an important reason for the development of consociational democracy in massively segmented societies like the Netherlands, Austria, Switzerland, and Lebanon "is the existence of external threats to the country."[3]

Despite these tendencies that favor the smaller democratic countries, severity of conflict does not appear to be related to size of country. Although democracies are less subject to severe conflict than nondemocracies, the severity of conflict among democracies also appears to be unrelated to size.

In Europe, however, constitutionalism and democratic institutions have been relatively less secure in three of the four larger countries that are now democracies than among most of the smaller democracies. For example, of the eleven smaller European democracies, only one, Austria, has had a change of regime since 1900 (its regime has changed three times) or an internal dictatorship; in contrast, of the four larger European democracies, France and Italy have changed regimes twice, and Germany three times. It is unnecessary to cite the lengthy dictatorships of Germany and Italy. However, the proportion of countries experiencing revolutions or civil wars since 1900 is about the same in both groups: three out of the eleven smaller European democracies and one out of the four larger European democracies. In both Finland and Ireland, to be sure, the struggles were associated with independence, but they were civil wars, nonetheless.

We conclude, then, that on the whole, representative democracy in a large country is neither more nor less prone to destruction from internal conflict than in a small country. In Europe, however, democratic institutions have been somewhat more stable in the eleven smaller European democracies than in the four large countries currently classed as democratic (though one of these, Britain, is a model of democratic stability).

Economic Capacities

To the extent that economies of scale exist, the larger a system is, the more it can take advantage of these economies; smaller sys-

[3] Arend Lijphart, *The Politics of Accommodation* (Berkeley, Calif., 1968), pp. 154–57.

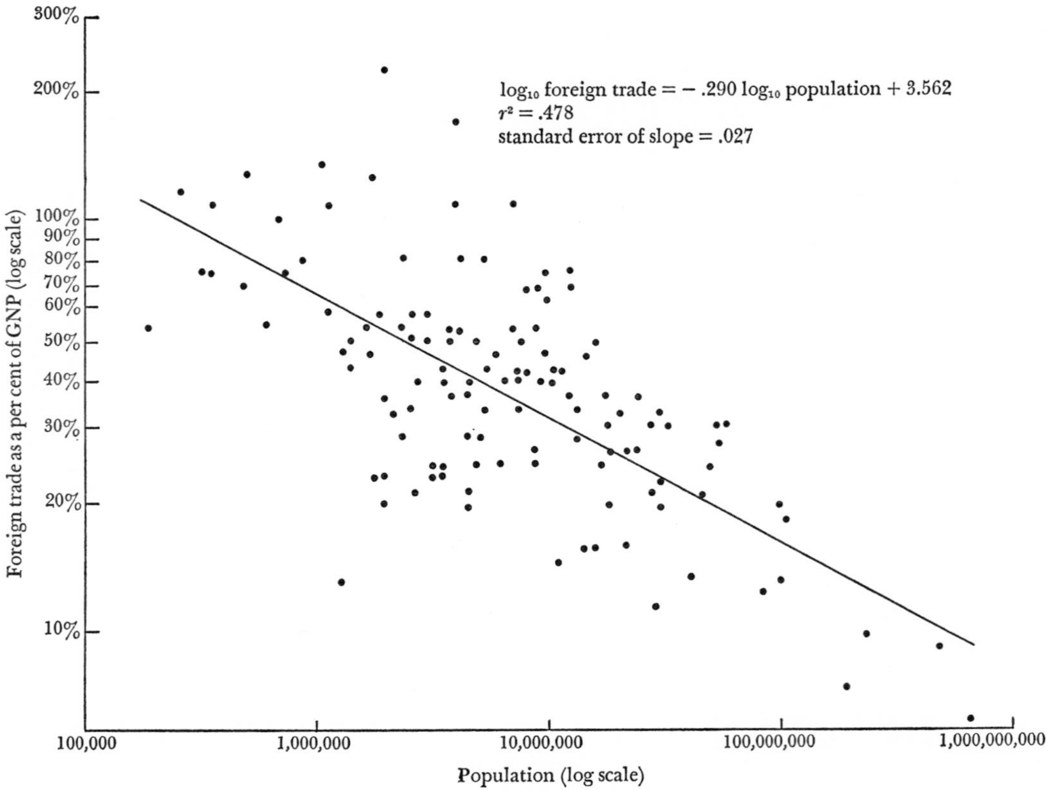

log₁₀ foreign trade = − .290 log₁₀ population + 3.562
r² = .478
standard error of slope = .027
Foreign trade as a per cent of GNP (log scale)
300%
200%
100%
90%
80%
70%
60%
50%
40%
30%
20%
10%
100,000
1,000,000
10,000,000
100,000,000
1,000,000,000
Population (log scale)

Fig. 7.1. Foreign trade and population among 124 countries, 1965.

tems are at a corresponding disadvantage. Are economies of scale significant?

It is scarcely open to doubt that the general principle is correct: economies frequently arise from specialization of labor and other resources used in producing goods and services. Since greater population (and territory) facilitate greater specialization, they help to generate economies of scale. Yet if classical economics enunciated this principle, it also enunciated a logical conclusion from it: the advantages of free trade. From this conclusion it follows in turn that economic "boundaries" do not need to coincide with political boundaries. By free trade, small political systems can achieve the same economies of scale as large systems.

Despite the fact that free trade is far from a reality, the argument does point the way to a partial solution to the problem for small systems—to engage in foreign trade. Hence we would expect that:

> In general, the smaller a political system the higher the proportion of foreign trade to total trade, particularly among systems with approximately the same income or product per capita.

Few relationships with size hold up more uniformly than this one. In 1965, for example, the ratio of foreign trade (imports plus exports) to GNP was 139.2 per cent for Trinidad and Tobago, 29.1 per cent for United Kingdom, 19.7 per cent for Japan, and 9.1 per cent for India. Figure 7.1 shows the relationship between foreign trade (expressed as a percentage of GNP) and population for 124 countries in 1965.[4] The fitted line shows that the population elasticity of foreign trade is −.290, indicating that an increase of one per cent in population is associated with a decrease of .290 per cent in foreign trade. (The standard error of the elasticity is .027, indicating that the result is statistically secure.) A similar regression, based on data collected ten years earlier for 80 countries, yielded the almost identical coefficient of −.270. Note the tremendous range in the level of foreign trade in the economy as

[4] Data based on Charles Lewis Taylor and Michael C. Hudson, *World Handbook of Political and Social Indicators*, 2d ed. (New Haven, 1972).

TABLE 7.1

Population Estimates of Some Large Medieval European Cities

City	Date of estimate	Population	Persons per hectare
London	1086	18,000	108
	1377	35,000	121
Milan	13th century	52,000	166
Naples	1278	27,000	133
Paris	1292	59,000	157
Padua	1320	41,000	117
Bruges	1340	25,000	58
Ghent	1356	60,000	93
Venice	1363	78,000	240
Bologna	1371	32,000	76
Florence	1381	55,000	107
	1424	37,000	73
Nuremberg	1449	23,000	165
Bourges	1487	32,000	289
Genoa	early 16th century	38,000	129
Barcelona	1514	31,000	118
Rome	1526	55,000	40

SOURCE: J. C. Russell, "Late Ancient and Medieval Population," *Transactions of the American Philosophical Society*, 48 (1958), Tables 63, 64, 65, presented in William Petersen, *Population* (New York, 1961), p. 351.

we compare the smaller countries, where the volume of such trade exceeds the GNP, with the larger countries, where it is less than 10 per cent of the GNP.

But of course the process is not automatic; obstacles to foreign trade may impede or prevent this solution to the economic problem of the small system. If so, the smaller system will be at a disadvantage, and may find it advantageous to associate itself politically with other countries. Thus economies of scale tend to erode the independence and autonomy of the smaller democracy by making it dependent—officially or not—on the actions of people outside the country.

Cultural Capacities

It is often thought that numbers bring cultural advantages, since the absolute numbers of geniuses or persons of high intellectual and artistic capacity must surely increase with the size of the population. As a cautionary note it is worth recalling that some of the city-states of greatest cultural creativity in Western history—Athens in the age of Pericles, republican Rome, Venice, Siena, Florence, to name a few—had populations about the size of present-day Iceland and were very much smaller than, say, Norway or Finland. The Renaissance began in what would now be considered small towns. (Table 7.1). Thus it is difficult to make a case for a relation between population size and creativity.

However, certain kinds of cultural performance require considerable specialization. Assembling a first-rate symphony orchestra or opera company is a matter of drawing performing artists from a large population. Even New York City does not man the Metropolitan Opera Company from its own native-born population. In performing arts that require large companies of specialists, it may be that large countries and large cities are more likely to assemble the needed skills than small countries or small cities. But even so, it does not follow that relative cultural advantage or deprivation is related to size. For tours and radio and television can bring the best performers to small countries or even small towns.[5]

[5] It would be interesting to know, for example, whether the percentage of the population who have attended an opera or a symphony concert varies at all with the size of the country. Otis Dudley Duncan reports for the United States that, although large and highly specialized museums are found only in cities of 250,000 or more, per capita attendance is actually inversely related to city size. "An Examination of the Problem of Optimum City Size" (Ph.D. diss., Chicago, 1949), cited by James Dahir, "What Is the Best Size for a City?," *American City*, August 1951, p. 104. See also Duncan's "Optimum Size of Cities," in P. K. Hatt and A. J. Reiss, Jr., eds., *Reader in Urban Sociology* (Glencoe, Ill., 1951), pp. 632–45.

EIGHT

Capacity for Independence and Autonomy

By entering into international trade, a small country may over-come the economic disadvantages of smallness; it may develop a relatively high GNP; it may excel in welfare programs and cultural opportunities. But in a lawless international world can a small country maintain its independence as well as a large country? Is it not more difficult for a small country to prevent its territory from being overrun and its national independence impaired or destroyed by a larger power?

Strategies for Survival

Since the advantages of large size and the disadvantages of small size seem too obvious to need emphasis, it may be useful to call attention to some ways a country with a small population may offset its disadvantages in relation to a larger country.[1]

Solution 1. A small country can reduce the differences between itself and larger countries in resources other than population. It may even surpass the more populous country in those resources.

Consider some of the possibilities: A small country may achieve a relatively high level of economic, social, and organizational development that compensates wholly or in part for its relatively smaller population. Thus Israel vs. Egypt. One highly important set of resources is that of morale, loyalty, courage, steadfastness,

[1] This is one of the few areas of our inquiry for which an extensive literature has recently developed. See Annette Baker Fox, *The Power of Small States* (Chicago, 1959); Burton Benedict, ed., *Problems of Smaller Territories* (London, 1967); Robert L. Rothstein, *Alliances and Small Powers* (New York, 1968); and David Vital, *The Survival of Small States: Studies in Small Power–Great Power Conflict* (London, 1971).

dedication, sacrifice. A small country may develop these to a very high level in comparison with the larger country. Thus, Israel vs. Egypt, North Vietnam vs. the United States.

A small country may concentrate heavily on its relationship with a larger country, whereas a larger country often dares not— or at any rate does not—concentrate so heavily on its relation with a smaller one. In the small country, the attention of political elites may be strongly focused on the relationship with the large country. In negotiations, the small country may send top-flight people who can act with great authority and discretion, whereas the larger country may send lower-echelon negotiators armed with little authority. The small country may concentrate its resources of intelligence, analysis, and planning, whereas in the perspectives of the large country the small country may be one of countless problems, and a relatively minor one at that.

In dealing with a larger country, a small country may specialize its resources to exploit the strengths and weaknesses of the larger country. Thus the North Vietnamese defeated the French and then frustrated the official aims of the United States Government by a specialized combination of political, military, and economic techniques that nullified much of the theoretically greater strengths of both larger countries.

Solution 2. The small country may raise the opportunity costs to the large nation of opposing the goals of the smaller country. That is, it may increase the advantages to the larger nation of supporting or yielding to its demands. In this strategy, the aim of the smaller country is not to defeat the larger nation but to manipulate it, to encourage and discourage.

This it may accomplish in several ways. The smaller country may systematically search for means of reducing or avoiding conflict with the larger country. It tries to avoid playing a zero-sum game with the larger country. It does not take conflict as given or inevitable but as something that can be reduced or avoided if creative thought is given to the problem. One way in which small nations often try to reduce conflict is, of course, by pursuing a policy of neutrality. The smaller country may also elevate the costs of military aggression (and thus make itself less vulnerable to threats) by developing a high level of military strength. Thus

Switzerland and Sweden have made it clear that military invasion would be a costly enterprise even to a large power. Third, the smaller country may increase its solidarity, mutual interests, and interdependence with the larger country by trade, tying its success to the prestige of the larger nation, or by becoming explicitly or implicitly an ally of the larger country. Finally, a smaller country threatened by one large country may increase its solidarity with another large country, thus creating a potential defender.

Bruce Russett has examined the seventeen cases between 1935 and 1951 where a major power "overtly threatened [a smaller country] with military force, and where the defender either had given, prior to the crisis, some indication of an intent to protect [the smaller country] or made a commitment in time to prevent the threatened attack."[2] Russett found that in six cases the "attacker" was dissuaded and in eleven it was not. In three of these cases the great-power "defender" went to war against the attacker, but in eight cases the defender backed down.

The last strategy, then, can hardly guarantee complete success. Nonetheless, both sets of solutions do provide a considerable array of strategies that, executed skillfully and in combination, may compensate for many of the disadvantages of smallness. In this century, the opportunity costs of toughness toward small countries have probably risen. Almost everywhere, independence movements have succeeded against larger colonial powers. And large nations have not escaped one of the chief consequences of being a great power: difficulty in staying out of a conflict. In fact, the experience of the European countries with war in this century suggests that the small countries have been no worse off than the large countries.

Chances of Survival

As we all know, these strategies of survival sometimes fail. Are the chances of a country's survival partly dependent on its size?

---

[2] Bruce M. Russett, "The Calculus of Deterrence," *Journal of Conflict Resolution*, 6 (1963), 97–108, esp. p. 98. Since all except one case (Berlin) involve small countries, we have substituted that term for Russett's "pawn," a word not easily stripped of other connotations. For a critique, see Clinton F. Fink, "More Calculations about Deterrence," *ibid.*, 9 (1965), 54–65.

In particular, do smaller countries have less chance of surviving than larger countries?

Thanks again to some recent work by Russett, it is possible to provide tentative answers to these questions. Russett's analysis indicates:

1. "There is no evidence that the largest states are proportionately either larger or smaller than 2,000 years ago."[3]

2. In recent decades, the only period for which adequate data are available, the proportion of small states, as measured by population, is much greater than the proportion of large states.

3. That the distribution is nearly lognormal is consistent with the interpretation that the rate of growth among states is random and not related to size. On this interpretation, then, large states do not grow in population (whether by births, conquest, or amalgamation) at any greater or lesser rate than small states.[4] However, the fact that the distribution *"departs slightly* from lognormality . . . leaves open the possibility that the very largest states may have grown faster."

4. However, if we examine data on rates of growth in the population of states from 1939 to 1965:

The hypothesis that big nations have been growing faster than smaller ones is unambiguously rejected. . . . Of the eight largest states, only China, and that barely (155%), had a growth rate higher than the rate achieved by the average nation overall (154%). Size does make some difference in growth, but opposite from the way expected. Growth rates for the *smallest* quartile of nations have been well above the average for nations as a whole.[5]

---

[3] Bruce M. Russett, "Is There a Long-Run Trend Toward Concentration in the International System?," *Comparative Political Studies*, 1 (1968), 119. For a somewhat different view, emphasizing the problem caused by the proliferation of the small, poor countries in Africa beginning in the early 1960's, see Jean-Luc Veilut, "Smaller States and the Problem of War and Peace: Some Consequences of the Emergence of Smaller States in Africa," *Journal of Peace Research*, no. 3 (1967), pp. 252–69.

[4] The model of random growth, independent of size, has been worked out by econometricians, who have demonstrated that a lognormal distribution is consistent with the model. Although their analysis was designed to test theories of concentration among business firms, the theory is perfectly appropriate to nations. Cf. the discussion in Russett, "Is There a Long-Run Trend?," pp. 105–7, and the works he cited in footnotes 4, 5, and 6.

[5] *Ibid.*, p. 115.

5. Moreover, there is greater variability in the rate of growth of large nations. "Apparently," Russett concludes, "a nation or empire has to *take chances in order to grow big* and to stay big, and thus is likely as a result to expand or shrink by a greater proportional amount than most countries."[6]

6. It is plausible that very small states, like very small businesses, would come into existence and die out more frequently than very large states. Russett's evidence lends only slight support to this hypothesis, and he does not himself propose it. Of the four states that ceased to exist between 1938 and 1968, the time he wrote his article,[7] all had populations of less than three million. During the same time period, however, 67 new states came into existence, and among these the proportion of small states is much larger than among old states. In fact, of the fifteen states that in 1968 had populations of less than one million, all but one (Luxembourg) were new. However, according to Russett, "above that level, there is no relation between size and post-1938 independence."[8]

We conclude, then, that a country's chances of survival do not depend significantly on its size.

Costs of Survival: Military Expenditures

Even if the smaller democracies can survive as independent states, are the costs of their survival too high? Specifically, are the costs of defending their independence against aggressors excessive? Since small countries face the possibility of aggression by much larger countries, it would seem a highly plausible conjecture that smaller countries should spend more per capita for defense than large countries. It is highly interesting, therefore, that precisely the contrary is true:

The *larger* a country's population, the more per capita it spends for defense.

The evidence relating population size to military expenditures as a proportion of GNP is strong. For most groupings of countries,

[6] *Ibid.*, p. 116.
[7] Estonia, Latvia, and Lithuania in 1940, and Zanzibar in 1964.
[8] *Ibid.*, p. 117.

TABLE 8.1

Simple Correlation Between Population (Log) and Military Expenditures
as a Per Cent of GNP (Log) for Various Groups of Nations in 1964

Group	Correlation	Number of countries
All nations	.43	113
Democracies	.64	32
Smaller European democracies	.83	11
Western nations	.80	21
African nations	.23	35
Latin American nations	.41	21
Far Eastern nations	.13	21
Near Eastern nations	.46	11
Richer nations	.68	30
Poorer nations	.33	83
Nations at war in last 10 years	.23	26
Nations not at war in last 10 years	.48	87

there are substantial correlations between size and military expenditures (see Table 8.1). Figures 8.1 and 8.2 show the relationship and a fitted line for all 113 countries of the world for which we had data and for the group of 32 relatively democratic countries. The fitted line for all 113 countries indicates that, whereas a country with a population of one million typically would spend about 1.5 per cent of its GNP on military support, a country of 100 million would spend about 5.3 per cent, or more than three times as much per capita. The responsiveness of military expenditures to population size is even greater in democratic countries. For relatively democratic countries, the fit is tighter, as Figure 8.2 indicates; population size explains over 40 per cent of the variance.

Are these results simply a consequence of a spurious correlation between size and some other variable? Would the relationship vanish, or drastically decline, if it were to take into account additional factors such as GNP per capita, or whether a country had recently been at war? As we saw earlier, GNP per capita is not significantly related to size; consequently the relation between population and defense expenditures should remain even if differences in GNP per capita were taken into account. Nor—during the past decade at least—has there been much relation between the size of a country and whether it has been involved in war; although it does appear that the larger countries have been some-

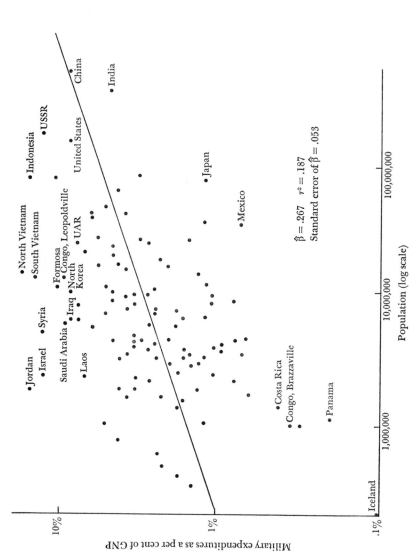

Fig. 8.1. Relation between population size and military expenditures for 113 countries.

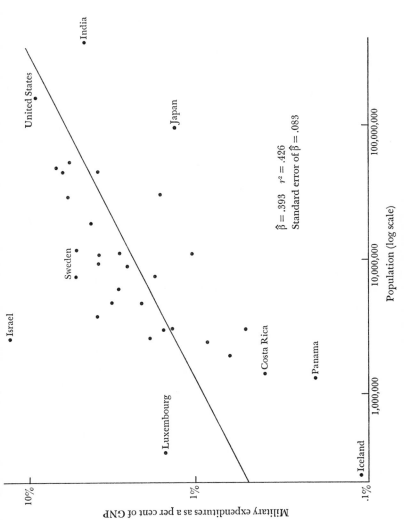

Fig. 8.2 Relation between population size and military expenditures for 32 democracies.

TABLE 8.2

Military Expenditures as a Per Cent of GNP: Multiple Regression Analysis

Category	113 nations		32 democracies	
	Regression coefficient	Standard error	Regression coefficient	Standard error
Population (log)	.214	.047	.376	.078
At peace last decade	−.443	.071	−.280	.174
GNP per capita (log)	.041	.059	.390	.126
R^2		.403		.590

what *more* likely to be involved in war.[9] It is not surprising then, that adding these two variables to the regression equations enables us to explain more of the variance in defense expenditures, but does not greatly lower our estimate of the impact of population. Fitted equations (Table 8.2)—which take into account a country's population, whether or not it has recently been involved in a war, and its GNP—statistically explain 40 per cent of the variation in military expenditures for all 113 nations and 59 per cent for democratic countries.

Since our findings run directly counter to the highly plausible conjecture that in order to maintain their independence small countries would have to spend more per capita than large countries, how do we account for the results?

1. It is possible that citizens and leaders in many smaller countries (there are notable exceptions) recognize that in a confrontation with a determined larger power they cannot maintain their independence exclusively by military means, no matter how much they might spend on defense. Suppose, for example, that an effective defense against invasion by a large country would require a small country to spend $10 billion a year. Suppose the

[9] The correlations among size, peace status, and GNP per capita are as follows:

	For 113 countries		For 32 polyarchies	
	GNP	Peace	GNP	Peace
Size	−.01	−.18	−.11	−.34
GNP		.13		.14

For the calculations represented here, size was defined as the logarithm of the population (population expressed in thousands); GNP, as the logarithm of the GNP per capita. Peace was defined as the condition of having been at peace for the ten years preceding the study.

small country's GNP is $5 billion. It could not possibly spend enough to prevent the large country from invading, if it were determined to do so. Hence the small country would have to search for a strategy of dissuasion that would not rely on its own military resources. With a GNP of $30 billion, however, a third country could choose to spend one-third of its GNP on defense against the large country's potential aggression, for an outlay of $10 billion would provide it with a relatively high degree of insurance against invasion.

2. If small countries enter into alliances with large countries, they can take refuge under the umbrella of the large country. The total expenditures by the alliance will far exceed what would be possible for the small country. However, the large country dare not reduce total expenditures on defense; yet ordinarily it cannot coerce the small country into maintaining defense outlays; hence the small countries in an alliance may be able to get by with lower defense expenditures per capita than the large, powerful leaders of the alliance. This appears to be the case with the NATO alliance, for example.[10]

3. Typically, the large country is more forceful, aggressive, dominant. Large states are leaders of alliances, centers of polarizing forces in the world, headquarters of empire. Their role induces them to make greater per capita expenditures on military matters in order to fulfill the requirements of the role. Where the small country concerns itself almost exclusively with countries that are on its borders, very large countries seek to defend themselves against other large countries no matter where they are located; and large countries play some part in every region of the world.

4. Some types of military goods are so inordinately costly that small countries may simply forgo them entirely: nuclear-powered submarines, intercontinental bombers, nuclear weapons, ICBMs and long-range missiles, for example.

There may be and there doubtless are any number of other explanations. But one thing is clear: smaller countries have lower

---

[10] Mancur Olson, Jr. and Richard Zeckhauser, "An Economic Theory of Alliances," *Review of Economics and Statistics*, 48 (1966), 266–79.

costs of survival than do larger countries, as can be measured by per capita expenditures for defense.

Costs of Survival: Losses from War

Nonetheless, it might be that the lower military expenditures of the smaller countries simply buy them less defense, and that smaller countries are more often overrun and seriously damaged by war. Although we do not have extensive data on this matter, a comparison of war losses among the eleven smaller and four larger European democracies would not, we believe, be unfavorable to the smaller countries. Of the four larger European democracies, three have been overrun, occupied, and severely damaged by foreign military forces twice in this century; and Britain suffered extensive bomb damage in World War II. Of the eleven smaller European democracies, only Austria, Belgium, and Luxembourg were overrun in both wars; Denmark, the Netherlands, and Norway were occupied in World War II; and Finland was invaded by both the USSR and Germany in that war. Iceland, Ireland, Sweden, and Switzerland suffered neither invasion nor other war damage. Except for Finland, military and civilian deaths from both wars were comparatively small in the smaller European democratic countries, whereas one or both wars took an extraordinary toll in the four larger countries.

In general, then, we conclude that the military costs of survival are not higher in smaller democracies than in large; if anything, they seem lower.

Independence and Autonomy

In Chapter 2 we emphasized that "democratic" political systems differ not only in the extent to which citizens may participate directly in making decisions but also in the extent to which the system is autonomous. In a completely autonomous democratic system, no one but citizens of the system would exercise power or authority over its decisions.

No democratic system has ever been completely autonomous. Nonetheless, in the fifth century B.C., Greek city-states were highly autonomous; typically only a citizen had any legitimate power (authority) over the decisions of the city-state. As everyone knows,

in the modern world, the power and authority of smaller systems
—villages, towns, cities, communes, states, provinces, regions—is,
de facto and de jure, regulated by and subordinate to power and
authority of the nation-state. During the second half of the twentieth century, the sovereignty of the nation-state itself has declined
as nation-states have begun to join supranational organizations
like the UN, the Common Market, NATO, EFTA, and Comecon,
and to accept binding limits on their sovereignty, like those contained in the Treaty on Nuclear Disarmament. If this process
continues, as it well might—as it must, we would insist, if a tech-
nological civilization and even mankind itself are to survive—
then in the future the nation-state may itself be transformed into
a "local government."

While it may be premature to speculate in detail about this
process, clearly it entails a loss in autonomy. Is this loss in autonomy—past, current, and future—likely to differ in any significant way among democracies according to size?

At first blush, it would seem that small countries are likely to
lose more of their autonomy than large countries: more likely in
the twenty-first century to become subordinate "local governments" in some larger polity. For the boundaries of small countries are in some cases too small to enable the people within the
country to deal satisfactorily with the problems they confront:
they are able to handle the problem satisfactorily only by cooperating in some way with people outside the boundaries of the
country.

At the risk of being pedantic, let us make clear what we mean
by boundaries that are too small. If, because of its boundaries, a
political system lacks authority to secure compliance from certain
actors whose behavior results in significant costs (or loss of potential benefits) to members of the system, then the boundaries of the
political system are smaller than the boundaries of the political
problem. One can think of numerous examples: the diffusion of
nuclear weapons, nuclear explosions, air and water pollution,
security from aggression, international trade, gold supply, monetary stability, foreign investment, international travel, exploita-
tion of seas, oceans, and continental shelfs, and so on. At subnational levels, of course, the list might be extended indefinitely.

As we have already hinted, one of the most important ways in which the autonomy of a small country is threatened is by its economic dependence. In order to develop and maintain a relatively high standard of living, the small country must necessarily go beyond its own boundaries in search of markets, and often in search of raw materials, labor, and capital investment as well. As a consequence, the small country is highly dependent on the behavior of foreign actors not subject to its authority.

When its boundaries are too small for a problem, in the sense just defined, what can a political system do? Consider some of the alternative strategies:[11]

1. The small system may adjust unilaterally to the behavior of the outside actor or actors. It may simply accept the costs of that behavior. Thus frugality and simplicity of life were stressed by Greek theorists as acceptable costs—indeed benefits—of the self-sufficiency of the city-state. In practice, however, the Greeks refused to accept the full costs of self-sufficiency: hence the Athenian Empire. Alternatively, it may search for unilateral adjustments that will reduce or eliminate these costs. For example, if up-river towns pollute the water supply, it may install a purification system.

2. The small system may try to achieve a mutual adjustment by negotiation or bargaining. This process may be implicit or explicit.

3. By cooperating with other systems, a small system may succeed in helping to create a superior authority with boundaries large enough to include the relevant actors. This authority may be a confederation in which enforcement is carried out by the constituent parts, each acting within its own boundaries; a federal system with direct enforcement of federal laws and rules by a central government, but with some autonomy constitutionally reserved to the constituent units; or a unitary system, with no constitutionally autonomous constituent units. Within the unitary system there are at least two possibilities: in one, territorial or other units such as local governments are granted some autonomy

11 See C. E. Lindblom's list of strategies in *The Intelligence of Democracy* (New York, 1965), pp. 33–34, 68, 84, for a richer categorization of kinds of adjustments.

with respect to some problems; in the other, no territorial or other units have any autonomy with respect to any problems. This is an extreme case. No democratic country—perhaps no country—denies all autonomy to subunits with respect to all problems. However, Italy and France are much closer to the extreme case than Switzerland, Australia, India, or the United States.

Luxembourg furnishes a convenient example of a country with boundaries too small for some of its problems.[12] Among the smaller European democracies Luxembourg is the smallest in area and the second smallest in population. The prosperity of Luxembourg is almost completely dependent on a single industry, steel, which accounts for 80 per cent of her GNP. This steel industry depends—and to an increasing extent—on outside sources of raw material: coke from Germany, the Netherlands, and Belgium; iron ore from various sources. Fifteen per cent of the labor force in the steel industry consists of foreigners, mainly Italians and Belgians: of the total labor force, 28 per cent are foreigners. As a completely landlocked state, Luxembourg depends heavily on foreign ports: Antwerp, Rotterdam, and Dunkirk. Culturally, too, the country depends on neighbors, for although both elementary and secondary schooling are compulsory and free, or virtually free, and although there are technical and commercial schools, Luxembourg has no university. Militarily, Luxembourg is obviously at the mercy of her neighbors. Her neutrality violated by Germany in both World Wars, the country was overrun, occupied, and, in World War II, badly damaged.

How, then, have the people of Luxembourg adapted to this dependence on actors outside their boundaries? To begin with, it is worth noting that in per capita GNP Luxembourg is below only Kuwait, the United States, Canada, and Switzerland. To develop and maintain this high level, she has had to enter into economic associations with larger states. Luxembourg was a member of the German Customs Union (*Zollverein*) from its inception in 1842 until the collapse of Germany in 1918. In 1922 she

---

[12] The description that follows is based on K. C. Edwards, "The Grand Duchy of Luxembourg," in Burton Benedict, ed., *Problems of Smaller Territories* (London, 1967), pp. 68–80.

entered into a customs union with Belgium; under this arrange-
ment Belgian currency also circulated freely in Luxembourg. In
the 1930's she signed trade agreements with the Scandinavian
countries, the Netherlands, and France. After World War II, she
joined Belgium and the Netherlands in establishing Benelux.
Luxembourg became a member of the European Coal and Steel
Community in 1952, the European Common Market in 1960.

Militarily, unilateral adjustment through neutrality having
failed in both World Wars, Luxembourg became a member of
NATO. She is also a UN member. She is now a member of Benelux, the Coal and Steel Community, the Common Market,
NATO, UNESCO, and the International Labour Organization,
among others.

Culturally, unilateral adjustment has been highly successful.
The lack of a university may even be an advantage. The youth
forced to attend universities in other countries not only broaden
their own experience but bring the benefits of an up-to-date train-
ing back to their own country. The limited utility of the mother
tongue beyond the frontiers means that German, French and,
increasingly English, are taught in the public schools. Everyone
is bilingual—or even trilingual. Letzeburgesch, German, and
French are all official languages, with French usually used in the
law courts, both the Luxembourg dialect and French in the parliament, and German in the popular press.

The quality of community life in Luxembourg is, in the judg-
ment of a sympathetic English observer, high:[13]

Another factor making for solidarity within the Luxembourg community . . . is the entire absence of an underprivileged class and the
fact that there are no really poor people. Although great variations
in income exist, the lower wages are well above those of many other
European countries and there are many forms of social security benefits.

Luxembourg thus presents a picture of a small fully-developed and
highly prosperous sovereign state. It is at the same time a closely-knit
community enjoying all the advantages of modern life unhindered
by social dissensions or political unrest. It exhibits the full and complex organization of a state many times its size and in this respect is

13 *Ibid.*, pp. 78–79.

probably unique even among advanced societies. Its democratic foundations and its international outlook afford some parallel with Switzerland. Its economy, developed on an industrial basis, is however far less balanced than that of Switzerland, and largely for that reason the Grand Duchy is a strong advocate of the wider economic integration offered by the European Common Market. She is fully aware, in fact, that her own destiny rests on increasing international collaboration in Western Europe.

Luxembourg cannot escape her dependence. Yet the ordinary person may be no more dependent on forces beyond his control than the ordinary American, Englishman, Frenchman, German, or Italian. In an interdependent world the forms for managing interdependence differ, but not the fact of interdependence itself. Large nations, like small nations, have lost and doubtless will continue to lose autonomy. The boundaries of even a very large nation are too small for some of the kinds of problems we listed a moment ago. France, Germany, Italy, and Britain are, like Luxembourg, members of the Common Market. Britain, Germany, and Italy are, like Luxembourg, members of NATO. If the United States is the dominant partner in NATO and a preeminent world power, like Luxembourg she finds her conduct hemmed in by the actions of others, a limit nowhere better dramatized than by her inability to defeat her government's opponents in Vietnam.

The point is not that there are no differences in the autonomy and power of nations, but that these are differences of degree, and not so great as to narrow the domain of representative democracy significantly in the smaller countries as opposed to the larger.

What is even more to the point, differences in the autonomy or power of a democratic country do not necessarily produce differences in the power of the individual citizen. In his capacity to participate effectively in decisions he cares about, a citizen of a large democracy is not inherently better off than a citizen of a small country—and sometimes he may be worse off. For if boundaries can be too small, they can also be too large.

Let us make clear what we mean by too large. If the application of uniform rules throughout a political system with given boundaries imposes costs (or loss of benefits) on some actors that could be avoided (with no significant costs to others) by nonuniform rules, then the boundaries of the political system are larger than the boundaries of the political problem.

In such a system, what avenues are available to people who suffer from the imposition of uniform rules? Posed this way, the question turns out to be very nearly the mirror image of the problem of being too small, except that now the problem begins precisely where our list of possible alternatives just ended. Roughly in order of increasing political difficulty, the alternatives for citizens adversely affected by uniform rules in a large system are:

Strategy 1. Adjust unilaterally, either by accepting the losses or by discovering an alternative that avoids them.

Strategy 2. Engage in mutual adjustment by negotiation and bargaining.

Strategy 3. Create a subordinate authority with boundaries small enough to include only the disadvantaged actors by means of administrative or legal autonomy within a unitary system (decentralization), a federal system with constitutional autonomy for the smaller constituent units (federalism), or a confederation (confederalism).

Strategy 4. In the extreme case, separation into an independent, sovereign system: the "nation-state."

Note that this last solution brings us back to the starting point: having solved the problem of boundaries that are too large for one problem, the new political system may now be confronted with the problem of boundaries that are too small for another.

Is There an Optimal Size?

Confronted by the disadvantages of boundaries smaller than the political problems it wishes to deal with, a political system may be driven successively from one alternative to the next, and in the process transform itself into a larger political system. But a larger political system, confronted by the disadvantages of boundaries larger than the problems it wishes to deal with by uniform rules, may be driven successively from one alternative to the next until it has transformed itself into a congeries of smaller political systems. Can we say, then, that there is any optimum size for a political system?

In our view, the answer is clearly no. Different problems require political units of different sizes. Practically every modern state recognizes this fact in practice: it meets the need for variation in the size of political units whenever existing boundaries are too large or too small by adopting one or more of the strategies just discussed.

In the representative democracies, however, theory has lagged behind practice. For about two thousand years, the dominant view was that the small city-state was optimal for democracy; for about two hundred years, the dominant view has been that the nation-state is optimal for democracy. Yet the plain facts of life are that neither is optimal for democracy.

Today and in the foreseeable future, people will live in a multiplicity of political units. Because democratic theorists, with notable exceptions, have focused on the problem of democratizing one sovereign unit—first the city, then the nation-state—they have overlooked the problem of democratizing a political system that consists of a collection of interacting units ranging from small primary associations in which direct democracy is at least theoretically possible to larger entities in which direct citizen rule is impossible. Rather than conceiving of democracy as located in a particular kind of inclusive, sovereign unit, we must learn to conceive of democracy spreading through a set of interrelated political systems, sometimes though not always arranged like Chinese boxes, the smaller nesting in the larger. The central theoretical problem is no longer to find suitable rules, like the majority principle, to apply within a sovereign unit, but to find suitable rules to apply among a variety of units, none of which is sovereign.

If our view is correct, citizens of democratic countries face a rather similar situation whatever the size of their country: they need to adapt democratic ideas and institutions to the fact that different problems are best met by units of different sizes. Very small countries like Luxembourg will enter into larger entities, like the Common Market, NATO, or a federal Europe. Very large countries like the United States and India will have to search for ways of creating or preserving smaller units like villages, cities, and states. Many smaller democracies — indeed, perhaps most democratic countries — will have to move in both directions: outward toward larger aggregates and inward toward smaller aggregates. As a smaller country like Luxembourg, let us say, moves outward and the aggregate system of which it is a part increases in size, the nature of democracy in that larger system will be affected by, among other things, the constraints and possibilities attendant upon increasing size. Conversely, in already large or giant systems, as attempts are made to preserve or discover smaller units thought to be more efficient in maximizing particular values, the nature of democracy in these smaller units will be determined, among other things, by the constraints and possibilities attendant upon decreasing size.

Epilogue

We have emphasized throughout this book how the historical search for a political system that would maximize both citizen effectiveness and system capacity has led to three radically different stages in the evolution of democratic units of government. For centuries the city-state was thought to be optimal for democratic purposes. Then the city-state was superseded by the nation-state, wholly in practice and partly in theory, as the proper unit for democracy. For some time now, the nation-state has been giving way to a complex, federated polity.

Ever since the shift away from the city-state some two centuries ago, theory has lagged behind reality. Or rather, theory appropriate to a preceding stage has twice been drafted into the service of the next. To cut into contemporary democratic ideas is therefore like penetrating strata from different times and circumstances, strata once geologically distinct, which over the centuries have become so intermingled that their original characteristics are hardly noticeable.

During the first two stages in the evolution of democratic theory and practice, it was commonly assumed that some specific type of unit—city-state, then nation-state—was optimal, in fact ideal, for democracy. When we first began to investigate the relation of size to democracy, like our predecessors we assumed, or at any rate hoped, that the fruits of our labors might be a definition or determination, in some fashion, of the optimal democratic unit. We have come to see how illusory that hope was. For it has become clear—and by now the reader will recognize it as a central perspective of this book—that:

> *No single type or size of unit is optimal for achieving the twin
> goals of citizen effectiveness and system capacity.*

For in the present world, and even more surely in the future,

> *Democratic goals conflict, and no single unit or kind of unit
> can best serve these goals.*

In particular, we have emphasized two sources of conflict: First,
the *effectiveness of the citizen* who is in concord with the pre-
ponderant majority of other citizens in his unit may well be maximized, as Rousseau thought, when the unit is small and homogeneous. The politics of homogeneity serve this citizen best. Yet in
such a unit the effectiveness of the dissenting citizen is minimized
by his difficulty in finding an ally, and by the weakness of political competition. The politics of diversity in the larger, more
heterogeneous unit may serve the dissenting citizen best. And yet
the same citizen may sometimes be in concord, sometimes in dissent.

Second, and more important, the goal of maximizing citizen
effectiveness on matters that are highly important to him can and
does conflict with the effort to maximize the *capacity of the system* (and hence ultimately, though in a different sense, the citizen's effectiveness) for dealing with these matters. In the extreme
case, a citizen could be maximally effective in a system of minimal
capacity for dealing with major issues (e.g. international violence)
or minimally effective in a system of maximal capacity for dealing
with major issues.

Now it may be said with some justice that what we have just
written has been known all along. Certainly the institutions of
democratic countries provide more than enough evidence that
"democracies" have in fact responded to the conflicting values
just described. Yet practice has far outstripped theory. And to
those who adhere to the sturdy simplicities of popular democratic
thought in the traditional mode, it is easy to conclude that practice is wrong, meaning undemocratic, because it violates theory.

The fact is, however, that democratic ideas as we have known
them up to now provide no adequate guide for discovering an
answer to the question: how can democracy be maximized in a

world unprecedented both in numbers and in the extent of human interdependence? Because it is disagreeable to conclude that maximizing one key aspiration in the democratic dream may badly damage another, the temptation, irresistible to many, is to reassert the old unflawed vision.

Nonetheless, if the capacity of ordinary human beings to exercise rational control over their lives is to be enhanced, and if interdependence among vast numbers of human beings is not to foster a miasma of legitimized domination, democratic theory will have to leap ahead and not jump directly into the past, as "new" or "radical" democratic thought invariably seems to do. An adequate new theory will have to be more than simply a conglomerate formed from the fragments of the old. Since we are unable to offer a full theory here, we conclude with a few suggestions bearing on that task.

To begin with, let us emphasize again the importance of directly confronting the deficiencies of democratic theory. Although it is conventional to conclude a work in the social sciences with a call for more research—meaning, usually, the analysis of more data—the crucial problems in the topic we have explored in this book arise from the inadequacies of normative-empirical theory bearing on democracy. It is our hunch that this deficiency is not going to be overcome either by mining the great theories of the past, hoping thereby to uncover a hitherto unnoticed view of precious metal, or by accumulating and analyzing new data. A highly interdependent world of several billion people —whether three, six, ten, or more billions—raises new problems of the most profound sort, and it seems to us doubtful that solutions will be found in theories formulated in and for profoundly different times, or in data analysis that charges ahead in the absence of new theoretical perspectives.

A more adequate theory would surely move from wings to center stage the neglected problem of political units and their interrelations. If our conclusion is correct that no single unit should be judged as optimal for democracy today—let alone for a range of human excellence broader than is encompassed by the purely political, in its limited, modern sense—then what units do we need, and how should they be related? To reply with federalism, as one might be tempted to do, is not so much to provide an answer as to restate the question, or, at best, to suggest a direction in which a part of the answer might be found.

It seems evident to us that among the units most needed in the world as it has been evolving lie several at the extremes: we need some very small units and some very large units. The very small units, like the Swedish communes under 8,000, once existed; but because of their inadequate system capacity they are rapidly vanishing. Very large units that transcend the parochialism and inadequate system capacity of the nation-state are evolving, but too slowly—quite possibly too slowly for human survival. If the giant units are needed for handling transnational matters of extraordinary moment, very small units seem to us necessary to provide a place where ordinary people can acquire the sense and the reality of moral responsibility and political effectiveness in a universe where remote galaxies of leaders spin on in courses mysterious and unfathomable to the ordinary citizen. At the same time that the transnational units will increase the capacity of the system to handle critical problems, and thus the collective effectiveness of a body of citizens, transnational units will also increase the ineffectuality and powerlessness of the individual citizen. As a consequence, the very small unit will become more, not less, important to the sense of effectiveness of the ordinary citizen. Yet finding space for truly significant activity in the very small unit is obviously going to be difficult.

Theory, then, needs to do what democratic theory has never done well: to offer useful guidance about the appropriate relations among units. This problem was virtually bypassed during the classical preoccupation with the city-state; interstate relations were literally anarchic. The nation-state merely transferred that anarchy to the relations of much larger units. And federalism is not so much a theory of inter-unit relations as a set of institutions, different from country to country, conveniently anchored in the nation-state—at least up to now.

One reason why federalism has been able to deal concretely with problems arising from relationships among the constituent units is that nationalism has helped to keep down severe conflicts of loyalties within the federal system by means of a moderately clear hierarchy of loyalties. The nation was generally held to be the unit of ultimate loyalty; a layer of intermediate units—states, provinces, cantons—came next; all other units, including municipal units, were definitely subordinate to the other two. Where a hierarchy of attachments did not fully develop, or broke down, conflicts of loyalties have led to serious confrontations, as in Canada, or to civil war, as in the United States. Yet how infinitely more difficult is the problem of loyalty in a complex polity that begins to transcend the nation-state!

If boundaries can be too small or too large, depending on the problem at hand, it might be thought that a theoretical solution would perhaps be found with a system having an indefinite number of units without permanently fixed boundaries, a system capable therefore of ready and infinite adaptability. This line of speculation seems to us, however, to promise one of those solutions of little theoretical interest and less practical value. Just as a central nervous system would quickly become overloaded by a proliferation of specialized organs constantly changing in size and shape, so the costs of communication and information, and therefore of control, would become overwhelming if citizens were confronted with an indefinite number of changing units. In fact, in complex political systems these costs already appear to be so high as drastically to impair citizen effectiveness. We have long since passed the time, if it ever existed, in representative democracies when an ordinary citizen could monitor all the functions and units with a large impact on his goals and policies. Even a legislator can no longer do so, and we probably have passed the point at which a full-time chief executive can do so.

Thus one task of democratic theory may be to specify not an optimal unit but an optimal number of units with comparatively fixed boundaries. The boundaries of each unit would be too small or too large for all functions assigned to it; but the costs of a small number of units with relatively fixed boundaries would be less than the costs of any larger number of units, or of constantly shifting boundaries.

A new democratic theory will also have to clarify the powers, obligations, and characteristics of citizens and leaders, including officials, in democratic units of different types. For example, some degree of specialization of attention will certainly be required, even under assumptions calling for a considerably higher level of political involvement on the part of citizens than is true now or perhaps has existed at any time in the past. We have seen how, with increasing size, specialization becomes necessary among leaders, but citizens must, and to some extent do, also specialize. Yet indefinite specialization, like an indefinite proliferation of units, would lead sooner or later—and may already have—to so much fragmentation as to create insuperable problems of coordination. Is responsibility for looking after the general, the larger wholes, to vanish entirely, or, finally rejecting the ancient ideal of a body of citizens concerned with "the general good," is this responsibility also to be lodged, knowingly, in a specialized group of citizens?

In order to catch up with the problem of the complex polity, it seems, democratic theory must (among other things) help one to decide, according to democratic or other acceptable criteria of political excellence, the optimal number of units, their characteristics, similarities, and differences, the nature of a good political life in each type of unit, and the proper relationships among them.

Index

Index

Africa, 73, 121n, 123
aggression, *see under* military, the
agricultural employment, 32, 104f, 107–8
Alemanni, 32
alliances between countries, 120, 127
ally in dissent, 90, 92f, 108, 138
Almond, Gabriel A., 47, 49n, 51, 55, 57, 62
American Constitutional Convention, 9f, 89
American Federation of Labor, 36
Amsterdam, the Netherlands, 57
area, 1, 17–19, 34f, 44–45, 48, 103, 105; and organizations, 36–40; mentioned, 27n, 106–7, 131
aristocracy, 5f, 17, 26
Aristotle, 4f, 6n
Articles of Confederation, 9
Asch, S. E., 90
associations, *see* organizations
Athens, 1, 22, 69–75 *passim*, 111, 117, 130
Australia, 17
Austria, 18f, 107, 112f, 128, 131
authority, hierarchy of, 36, 78
autonomy, 2–8 *passim*, 18–28 *passim*, 43, 55, 60, 111, 116; of subleaders, 78, 87; independence and, 128–34

Barcelona (city-state), 116
Barotse tribe (Africa), 73
Belgium, 18, 32, 107, 112, 128, 131f
Benelux, 132
Bologna (city-state), 116
Bourges (city-state), 116
Brazil, 17
Bruges (city-state), 116
bureaucracy, 36, 77–78
Burgundians, 32

Canada, 3, 17, 131, 141
centralization, *see* decentralization
chairman's problem, 71–72
Chile, 60, 82

China, 17, 111, 121
churches, number of, 36
citizen effectiveness, 20–25, 29, 80, 84, 137f, 140f; and size, 1, 6, 86, 89–90, 108–9, 133; participation and, 41–66, 133
city-states, 4, 6, 61, 73, 110f, 117, 128, 140; as locus of democracy, 8–12, 20f, 24f, 79, 135, 137
civil war, 113, 141; United States, 36, 141; Finland, 50; Ireland, 112
coalition of dissent, 90, 97
code of behavior, 92f. *See also* norms, collective
Comecon, 129
communication, 15, 36, 38f, 66–88, 95, 108f, 141
Communist party (Finland), 50
community: sense of, 3, 15; loyalty to, 14; Luxembourg as, 132
confederation, *see* federalism
conflict, 13, 89–109, 111–13, 119f
conformity, *see* norms, collective
control of government, popular, 2, 8, 9n, 11–15, 17, 25, 28, 65. *See also* leaders
Converse, Philip E., 47
costs, 27–28, 93–94, 119–20, 127–28, 130, 134; of participation, 41f, 45, 55, 108f; of communication, 66–68, 80, 108f, 141
creativity, 117
culture: diversity of, 31, 33f; effect of, 44, 46, 53, 80, 88, 111, 115–18, 132
customs union, 131f

decentralization, 3, 11–13, 36–40 *passim*, 60, 79, 134
defense, *see* military, the
de Jouvenel, Bertrand, 71–72
democracy, 25–29, 36, 61, 63–66, 79, 87, 135–39; grass-roots, 2, 12; classical view of, 4–13 *passim*; direct, 8f, 11, 17, 22–27 *passim*, 46–47, 89, 135; participatory,

12, 21f, 69–70; dimensions of, 20–25; primary, 79; consociational, 113
democracy, representative, 8, 17–19, 26f, 40, 89, 113, 133, 135, 141; criteria for, 22–23; federalism in, 37, 79; centralization in, 37–38; participation in, 46–47, 87–88; and communication, 74, 87–88
democratic systems, 1, 57, 60, 97, 113, 115, 123, 135–36, 138; participation in, 41–42, 45, 53, 57, 60f, 108; effectiveness in, 51–53, 57, 60, 109; autonomy of, 60, 122–33 *passim*; communication in, 70–71, 73, 76, 81, 84, 108; conflict in, 91, 94, 96, 108; diversity in, 100, 106, 112f; system capacity of, 110f
democratic theory, 8–15, 22, 73, 79, 84; classical view of, 4–8, 17, 21, 28, 135–42 *passim*
Denmark, 112, 128
Destutt de Tracy, Antoine, 9, 27
dictatorship, 36f
differentiation, *see* specialization
dissent, 89–92, 98, 108, 132, 138
diversity, 9–10, 13–14, 31–35, 38, 42, 89, 91–112 *passim*
division of powers, 6
Dublin, Ireland, 51
Dun and Bradstreet, 36
Dupeux, Georges, 47

economic development, 101, 103, 111–18 *passim*
education, 32, 44, 46f, 53, 62, 84, 95, 103, 132
effectiveness, *see* citizen effectiveness
EFTA, 129
Egypt, 118–19
elections, *see* voting
England, 12, 25. *See also* United Kingdom
English language, 132
ethnic diversity, 34
Eulau, Heinz, 97
Europe, 2, 8, 95, 112f; federal, 2, 136; and war, 120, 123, 128; mentioned, 131ff. *See also* democratic systems *and countries by name*
Europe, United States of, 2
European Coal and Steel Community, 132
European Common Market, 79, 129, 132f, 136
Eyestone, Robert, 97

factionalism, 10–11, 89, 112
Far East, 3, 114, 119, 123, 133
federalism, 2, 8ff, 37, 79, 130, 134, 137, 140–41
Federalist, The, 10, 26
Finland, 18, 32, 47–50, 112f, 117, 128
Florence (city-state), 116–17
France, 12, 18, 32, 47f, 113, 119, 131ff

French language, 32, 132
French Revolution, 6, 11–12

Garibaldi, 12
Geneva, Switzerland, 1
Genoa (city-state), 116
geography, 4, 18, 34, 37
German Customs Union, 131
German language, 32, 132
Germany, 8, 18, 113, 128, 131
Germany, West, 32, 47, 49, 52–59, 131, 133
Ghent (city-state), 116
Girod, Roger, 105
Glaucon's problem, 69–70, 72
government, 12, 23, 43, 52f, 72, 84; sub-units, 23, 37–38, 40; local *vs.* national, 43, 52–62, 65, 80; impact of, 55–57, 59. *See also* democracy; democratic systems
Great Britain, 95, 112f, 128, 133; 18th-century, 8, 25; 19th-century, 12. *See also* United Kingdom
Greece, ancient, 4–5, 9, 17f, 110–11, 128, 130
gross national product, 19, 114f, 118, 122f, 126–27
groups, small, *see* small-group theory

Hamilton, Alexander, 9n, 10
heterogeneity, 9–10, 13–14, 91–98 *passim*, 105f, 109, 112. *See also* diversity
historical factors, 31–35, 53, 95, 106, 112
Hofferbert, Richard, 108
homogeneity, 13, 44, 85, 91–94, 97, 105, 109, 112, 138

Iceland, 76, 81, 94, 112, 117, 128
income, 31, 84f, 132
independence, 111–22 *passim*, 126, 128–34. *See also* autonomy
India, 1, 17–18, 81, 114, 131, 136
indifference curves, 24
industrialization, 19, 32, 95, 100f
interest groups, 39f. *See also* factionalism
International Labour Organization, 132
Ireland, 51f, 76, 112, 128
Israel, 82, 118–19
Italy, 4, 12, 45–60 *passim*, 113, 131, 133

Jackson, Andrew, 12
Jacobins, 6, 11–12
Japan, 3, 115
Jefferson, Thomas, 9, 26–27

Kuwait, 131

Labor Party (Norwegian), 48
Landsgemeinde, 22
language, 31–35, 112, 132
Latin America, 17, 51–59 *passim*, 123
leaders, 77, 79f, 87–88, 142; responsiveness

of, 15, 22, 29, 66, 74, 89; as group
   representative, 71–72, 84–86, 109
Lebanon, 82, 113
Letzeburgesch, 132
liberals: in England, 12; in Netherlands,
   101, 103
Lijphart, Arend, 51, 113
Lincoln, Abraham, 12
London, England, 3, 18; city-state, 116
Lorwin, Val R., 32, 112
loyalties, 8, 14, 119, 141
Luxembourg, 76, 122, 128, 131–33, 135f

Madison, James, 9n, 10–11, 26–27, 39,
   89, 112
Mazzini, 12
Mexico, 51–59 *passim*
Michelet, 12
Milan (city-state), 116
military, the, 36, 38–39, 55; Roman, 4;
   aggression by, 111–13, 119–20, 122, 129,
   132; expenditures for, 122–28
Mill, James, 9n
Mill, John Stuart, 12
modernization, 32, 35f, 95–96
Montesquieu, 6–10, 26, 89, 91, 112

Naples (city-state), 116
nationalism, 8, 12, 141
nation-states, 2, 6f, 28, 73, 80, 95, 129, 134;
   emergence of, 7–9, 12; as locus of
   democracy, 20–26, 61, 79, 135, 137; very
   large, 79, 140f; breakdown of, 110
NATO, 127, 129, 132f, 136
Near East, 82, 118–19, 123
Netherlands, the, 1f, 18, 82, 95, 107, 112f,
   128, 131f; diversity in, 32, 105, 112;
   participation in, 45–53 *passim*, 57, 59;
   party competition in, 98–103, 105
neutrality: in small group, 94; as survival policy, 119; in Luxembourg, 131f
New England townships, 22f, 27n
New York City, 3, 117
norms, collective, 14, 41–42, 90, 92f
Norway, 1, 18, 48ff, 107, 112, 117, 128
Nuclear Disarmament, Treaty on, 129
Nuremberg (city-state), 116

officials, *see* leaders
opinion survey, 78
organizations, 32–40, 44, 48–49, 59–60, 64,
   91–99, 108f, 118; "span of control," 36,
   39; supranational, 129

Padua (city-state), 116
Paris (city-state), 116
parliaments, 25, 76f, 80–83
participation, citizen, 6, 13, 41–66, 71,
   73, 79, 99, 128; and effectiveness, 21–23,
   25, 46–49, 133; costs of, 41f, 45, 55, 108f

partisanship, 49–50, 97ff, 105. *See also*
   political parties
Pericles, 5, 74–75, 116
Philosophical Radicals, 12
Plato, 4f, 6n, 17
"Plumber's Law," 39, 91, 93
pluralism, 34, 112
polis, 4–5, 17
political parties, 48–50, 81, 95–109, 138
polyarchy, defined, 27n
population, 1, 3, 5–7, 17–20, 27n, 33n;
   growth, 1ff, 76, 80–82, 121–22; density,
   17ff, 34, 42, 44–45, 63–65, 86, 89, 95–105
   passim, 112; distribution, 18, 20n, 42;
   and diversity, 33–35, 86, 93, 95; and
   organizations, 36–60; participation and,
   42–51 *passim*, 63f, 86; and communication, 66–67, 77, 80, 86; political parties
   and, 99ff, 103, 106–8; and system capacity, 110ff, 114–16; and autonomy,
   118, 121–26, 131
pressure groups, 98
professionalization, 33, 75–76, 84, 87
Protestants (Netherlands), 101, 103

Reform '66 (Netherlands), 46
religion, 31, 33ff, 101ff, 112
representation, 8–11, 25–28, 73–76, 89;
   proportional, 46, 100, 106
representativeness, *see* leaders
republics, 4, 6–12, 26–27, 27n–28n, 89
responsiveness, *see under* leaders
Roman Catholic Church, 101
Rome, ancient, 4, 26, 116–17
Rousseau, 1, 4, 6ff, 26n, 43, 89, 91, 138;
   general will, 6, 11–12
Russett, Bruce M., 120–22

San Francisco Bay Region, 97–98
San Marino, 1
Scandinavian countries, 132. *See also by
   name*
security, 13, 113, 129
self-sufficiency, *see* autonomy
Siena (city-state), 117
size, 1, 9–15, 17–29, 137–38, 141; and
   diversity, 31–35, 91–92, 95, 97f; organizations and, 35–40, 96–98; and
   participation and effectiveness, 41–65,
   80, 89, 108f; communication and, 66–
   88; and conflict, 89–109, 120; system
   capacity and, 110–17; and autonomy,
   118–36
small-group theory, 13, 70–71, 90
socialists: in Sweden, 86; in Netherlands,
   101, 103
socioeconomic factors, 19f, 31–36, 40,
   95–96
sovereignty, 2, 6–7, 21, 23. *See also*
   autonomy

specialization, 15, 32–33, 39, 95, 100, 106,
142; of political leaders, 76–77, 79, 84,
87, 142; and system capacity, 114, 117
Spirit of the Laws, The, 6
survival, 20, 118–28
Sweden, 1, 32, 95, 107, 112, 140; Local
Government Research Group study,
63–65, 84ff, 98f; representation in, 82–
83, 85f; survival by, 120, 128
Swiss League, 8–9
Switzerland, 1, 18, 22–23, 37, 113, 120,
128, 131, 133; diversity in, 32–34,
103–5
system capacity, 20–25, 29, 108–17, 137f,
140

Tampere, Finland, 47–50
territory, 4–13 *passim*, 17–20, 42, 93f, 112,
130–31; and specialization, 77, 79, 115
time, 68–76, 80
trade, 114–16, 118, 120, 129, 132
trade unions, 36, 39
Tyler, John, 26n

understanding, sense of, 54f, 60
UNESCO, 132
Union of Soviet Socialist Republics, 17f,
111f, 128

unions, trade, 36, 39
United Kingdom, 1, 18, 47–60 *passim*,
112ff, 128, 133. *See also* Ireland
United Nations, 129, 132
United States, 1–3, 12, 17–18, 37, 95, 136,
141; early history of, 6, 8–11; diversity
in, 30, 32, 36, 106–8; participation and
effectiveness in, 44–63 *passim*; communication in, 73, 76f, 79, 81; system
capacity of, 111, 117n; and Vietnam,
119, 133; autonomy in, 131, 133
United States Congress, 73, 76f
urbanization, 1, 19, 32, 34, 62, 95–108
passim

Venice: Republic of, 26, 111; city-state,
116–17
Verba, Sidney, 47, 49n, 51, 55, 57, 62
Vietnam, 119, 133
voting, 3, 5, 13, 42–47, 59–60, 73; turnout,
44–45, 47, 57, 59–61, 79; and party
competition, 100f, 105, 107–8

war, 120, 123, 126, 128. *See also* civil war;
World War I; World War II
Westerståhl, Jörgen, 63n
World War I, 19, 131f
World War II, 128, 131f